ROCKABYE

✿ FROM WILD TO CHILD

Rebecca Woolf

SEAL PRESS

ROCKABYE

FROM WILD TO CHILD

Seal Press
A Member of the Perseus Books Group
1700 Fourth Street
Berkeley, CA 94710

Library of Congress Cataloging-in-Publication Data is available.

ISBN-10: 1-58005-232-0
ISBN-13: 978-1-58005-232-0

Cover Design by Susan Koski Zucker
Interior Design by Domini Dragoone
Printed in the United States
Distributed by Publishers Group West

FOR MY MOTHER AND MY SON

CONTENTS

"MENTAL FIGHT MEANS thinking against the current, not with it. It is our business to puncture gas bags and discover the seeds of truth."

—*Virginia Woolf*

INTRODUCTION
On Unplanned Pregnancy, for a Friend

DEAR FRIEND,

I would congratulate you on your pregnancy but I know you don't know how to say thank you right now, and that's okay. It's okay to be afraid. It's okay to mourn your single life and all your yesterdays, to look in the mirror and find yourself unrecognizable, to feel as if you're sleepwalking, sick to your stomach, speechless. There's nothing wrong with long silences and blank thoughts. There is nothing wrong with being afraid.

Forget morning sickness and weight gain and childbirth—the hardest part is right now. Today. Trying to understand the largeness of the situation, accepting the truth, trusting the double lines on the pregnancy test, saying aloud "I'm pregnant." There is nothing more difficult than unknowingly crossing the line, becoming two people overnight, touching your body and coming to terms with the fact that inside, a face is forming and, with it, a new world, a giant door that leads to everywhere, a wild jungle and OH MY GOD. Yes, everything will be different now.

When I first found out I was pregnant I couldn't say it aloud for several days. I choked on my words and swallowed air in their place. It wasn't until I had written the words down on paper one hundred times that I could finally repeat them aloud. *I. Am. Pregnant. Me, pregnant. I am going to have a baby. There is something alive in my body, and one day it will have a name. Holy shit! How is that possible?*

Give yourself time. You do not need to tell anyone if you don't want to. You don't need to be excited yet. You don't need to plan your future. You only need to plan for the moment. For today. Get yourself through today, and tomorrow will be easier. And then next week—next week you will feel differently. I promise. The first few days are the hardest—the most confusing, like in a dream.

It takes time to feel comfortable with a new friend, to get along with a roommate, to trust a stranger—and so with the child growing inside you, it is much the same. The key to any healthy relationship is time and faith and honesty. Be honest with yourself, and do not be afraid to be afraid.

Pregnancy was the most amazing physical experience of my

life. I cannot imagine never experiencing those forty weeks of creation, the changes and the swelling of self. I cannot imagine my body without its stretched tattoos and belly flab. I cannot imagine my life without Archer.

I looked into your eyes today, and I so remembered the feeling. I remembered the fear, lack of control, and loss of power. I remembered what I was wearing when I found out, the way my hair looked, auburn roots coming through my black dye-job. Roots that have since grown out completely. I remember feeling like my life was over. The end.

And I looked into your eyes, at your hair, and thought, You too will remember this moment. You will remember what you were wearing, faded workout pants and sneakers, and recall the banana clip in your hair. You will remember the smell of my car when I picked you up. You will remember the way the world suddenly looked different. A shade off. A new tint. You will remember it like it was yesterday—a turning point in your life.

I dropped you off at home so you could be alone with your thoughts and your body and your boyfriend. And when I came home I looked into Archer's eyes and saw all that love—my perfect son—and I thought of you, because soon, thirty-two weeks from now, you will feel like you just made a wish and it came true. You will look into the eyes of your child and see a beginning—*the* beginning—and you won't believe you thought this new life meant saying goodbye to yourself. And I will congratulate you again, and in a whole new way, you won't know what to say. You will be speechless.

Most definitely your life has changed directions. Most definitely I know that you will find your way.

ALWAYS YOUR FRIEND,
REBECCA WOOLF
FEBRUARY 2008

HOLY SHIT,
I'm Pregnant

❧

I MUST BE DRUNK or on drugs or dreaming. My breasts are not sore and the nausea I've been feeling is just a weeklong hangover. I had a lot to drink last week at the Three of Clubs. Five rounds or so.

There is no way I can be pregnant.

I light up a cigarette and lean out the window of my bedroom. My hands are shaking. My tattoos itch. They always itch when I'm nervous, rising up from my skin like swollen bug bites.

"I'm not pregnant," I say aloud.

My roommate knocks on my bedroom door. "Are you talking to me?"

I don't answer. I quickly hide the pregnancy test and its double yellowed lines under a towel and mumble something about going for a drive as I trip out the door.

I roll down the windows of my silver Volkswagen and merge onto Santa Monica Boulevard. The summer wind is thick with smog and mariachi music. It's Friday night. My friends and I will be meeting at the bar in an hour. I can't be pregnant. I'm meeting Mitzi and Terra for vodka tonics and darts at ten o'clock.

I pull into Rite-Aid and forget to lock my car. Sometimes I forget to press the button on my keychain. Sometimes I press the button and it doesn't lock. *Damn Volkswagens.* I pull my hooded sweatshirt over my head and wrap my hair around my neck. I don't want anyone to notice that I was just here, not even an hour ago. Twice in one night. Buying pregnancy tests from the Asian man with the thick accent and knowing eyes.

I pace near the explicit materials aisle, condoms *ribbed for her pleasure* beside the Astroglide beside the Clearblue Easy Pregnancy Tests beside the calling cards. I can't figure out what calling cards are doing next to the condoms. *When the condoms break, when the lube dries, when I'm feeling sad, I simply make a long-distance call to Japan and then I don't feel so bad.*

I make up songs in my head when I'm afraid, and right now I'm scared out of my mind. I want to break out of the moment, climb up the walls and hide behind the fluorescent lights in the ceiling so I can watch women in my position and see what they do. See if they notice the calling cards that methodically line the isle of horror. *We never used a condom. It was stupid.*

I can feel the eyes of wandering patrons, people pretending not to stare. I know they are pretending not to stare because I do the same thing. We all have eyes in the backs of our heads. We all lead double lives as spies.

Why couldn't we have used a condom? Why do I do such stupid things?

I casually reach for the e.p.t. test, knocking over several tubes of K-Y Jelly. I restock the boxes on the shelf and make my way to the register.

"You were just here, yes?" the pharmacist asks.

"Yeah but I bought a generic test. It was cheaper. I have to be sure."

He nods. "Is okay?"

I nod back. "I'm fine. It must have been broken. I just want to buy a few extras to make sure. I don't know which brand is the most trusted."

I can't be pregnant. I'm only twenty-three.

It seems impossible for me to be pregnant now. All of the years of drunken sex with strangers, forgotten birth control pills, weekend trips blurred from substance abuse, my year of so-called nymphomania. *My name is Rebecca and I'm a sex addict.* But I wasn't a sex addict. I was just lonely.

I'm only twenty-three.

I sneak into the house, past my roommate Frank, who is outside smoking cigarettes on the patio. Candles lit around him, he is laughing, flirting with his boyfriend on the phone. I walk slowly up the tiled stairs, invisible. Everything moves in slow motion, my dog's wagging tail, the cat behind the vase on the landing. Light and shadows change shape like the eyes of a jack-o'-lantern. *When I wake up, this will all be forgotten. I am sleepwalking is all. Only a dream.* My hands are shaking. I have to pee. But maybe if I hold it in forever I'll never know the truth. I'll hold my breath and everything will be the same. Cigarettes in bed and late-night dinners at Toi Thai on Sunset and a sleepover with my boyfriend who will never know—because I will never know. *Hold it all in. It's worth the pain.* I don't want to have to pee on four more pregnancy tests to know the truth.

I sit down on the worn toilet seat, spread my legs, and aim for the tab on the plastic stick. And then I do it again and again until there are six peed-on tests in a neat little row and the results appear clear as day, like twelve painted lines:

(II) (II) (II) (II) (II) (II)

I make sure the row is straight and there is an equal amount of space between each test. I clean the sink, wipe the toothpaste splatter off the mirror with wet toilet paper, and apply lipstick and perfume. I adjust the tests to control the chaos. I drag my finger across the urine-soaked vanity table and write my name in piss and eye-shadow dust.

For two hours I hide under the sink, folded up like origami, watching the clock move its rusted hands around the face of time.

Everything is moving as if underwater, slowly dancing with the current that I can recognize only as fear. I am so afraid, I could die right here in this spot on the floor, up to my ankles in dog hair and dirty clothes, beside the toilet I forgot to flush. I could fall on my face over and over until I become unrecognizable, too swollen to know that I'm the one carrying the burden.

I flush the toilet.

All I can think of when I look up at the water marks on the ceiling is that I'm not alone. I have never felt so alone in my life, and yet I suddenly feel so abnormally full of life. I immediately recognize that there is something inside of me, surviving. Something so tiny. Something so huge. *Hold me closer, tiny dancer.* I wish I had a different song stuck in my head.

"What the hell am I supposed to do now?" I ask.

Except I'm the only one who can answer that. It's up to me to figure out if I am willing to change my life. Little girl all grown up. People to see and things to do and distant lands to travel. Books to write and magazines to query and ideas to explore on my own. If only I could disappear first. How can I be pregnant with anything but ideas?

I'm angry. At myself for being so careless. At my body for being alive, unpredictable, female.

And the anger turns into rage. The pregnancy tests go flying across the room, against the walls and the mirrors and out the window. And the neighbors next door are fighting again and the cars are honking as they run the stop sign out front and the dogs outside are still barking, harmoniously calling out against the Santa Ana winds.

If only I could blow away.

I light another cigarette. I put it out. One after another I light them on fire, trying with all my might to inhale but I can't do it. And I knock the ashtray over trying to put out one more cigarette, lit and wasted. I never waste cigarettes and I dig through my make-up drawer to find a pen and I pull a receipt out of the trash bin and I write as many question marks as I can fit on the tiny yellow paper:

??

Frank is knocking on the door.

"Bec? You okay in there?"

But instead of lying to him I say nothing because I know he will know to come find me, which he does. He opens the door and sees the mess I've made, that I am shaking under the sink with e.p.t. tests in every corner of the room.

The dogs from next door stop barking. The city holds its breath. The whole wide world pauses. Frank picks up one of the pregnancy tests.

"Fuck."

"Fuck," I echo. "Fuck, fuck, fuck!"

"You're pregnant," he says, the same fear in his own eyes.

I shake my head, climb out from under the sink, and cry in his arms.

"What will you do now?"

"I don't know. I need to tell Hal."

I don't know how I'm going to tell him. Hal and I have only been dating for four months and I am afraid. Scared out of my wits. But I love him and when I close my eyes I think of him beside me in bed, smoking cigarettes and beating me at truth or dare in the "tree house," which is what he calls my bedroom because all you can see when you look out the windows are the rubber trees spilling onto the street, overgrown and pressed against the glass.

I dare myself to tell the truth, to wait until I stop shaking so I can get in my car and drive over to his house and sit down with him so we can talk about this like adults. I will not be hysterical. I will be collected. Like couples are in the movies or on television. Girl gets pregnant. Boy holds girlfriend's hand as she breaks the news. Boy shakes his head and hugs girl. Roll credits.

An hour of waiting and I'm still shaking. I realize now that the shaking isn't going to stop. Maybe one day but not tonight. I hold on to Frank's hand and together we walk down the stairs. I don't have any shoes on because I can't think where they are right now or how to go about putting them on. I walk barefoot through the kitchen and out the door.

Frank kisses my cheeks. "Good luck."

I get into my car and reverse into traffic, driving slowly, with snot in my nose, hyperventilating. I turn left on Fairfax and then onto Melrose. I get every green light on my way to Hal's house.

The lights are on in the living room and I watch the many shadows of his roommates, bending and flexing against the window curtains as the colors change pink to green from the rainbow glow of the TV. I am frozen to my seat. I cannot go inside. Not right now. Not with his roommates home and the makeup smeared across my face.

I call him from the safety of my car.

"Hello?"

I tell Hal between asthmatic wails to come outside, that I am outside. Please come outside.

The drape opens. Our eyes meet through the window and then the drape closes and the front door of the house swings open and he comes to me, white-faced.

I try to speak but I can't so instead I go on with charades and hysterics and I wish I had a piece of paper so I could write "I'm pregnant" like in that scene in *Wild at Heart.* I wish the director could just call "CUT" so I could stop trying to make sense. I wish I didn't choke every time I opened my mouth.

I point to my belly.

"You're pregnant?"

I nod.

And then he holds me and I twitch and choke on his shoulder and I shake my head and he pulls away for a moment just to say, "We're in this together." And I smile because suddenly I'm not alone, *we're in this together now,* and I tell him that I love him and after an hour of squirming in his arms I finally calm down.

"We will figure this out. Whatever happens, okay? It's going to be alright."

And I believe him. I nod and pull my hair out of my face and believe with all my might.

For the next ten days, I barely sleep, and when I do, I dream of darkness. I dream of hollow days and sunken eyes and black sunsets. I dream of broken hearts and the fist that holds my chest together, opening and closing and blowing itself up. I dream of bodies without faces and stick figures twisted like yarn. I dream of giving birth to myself.

For the next few days everything is different. I can't stop tripping over my feet or the dog's tail or the invisible holes in the hardwood floor. My world is booby-trapped. Land mines exploding at every turn and I feel for my limbs to make sure they're still there.

I think only of our choice. We both want to talk about what to do, but neither of us can articulate our needs, our wants, our questions, so instead we fight and cry and argue and throw household items at the wall. Plastic cups and ashtrays and coasters that roll across the room like little tires.

"If we keep the baby, everything will change," he says.

"If we don't keep the baby, I will not be able to be with you anymore," I respond.

"I will leave the choice up to you, then," Hal says. "It's your call."

I don't want to be alone.

I make an appointment with my doctor. I go out to the bar and do not drink. I say no when my coworkers offer me cigarettes. I rub my belly. I curse my belly. I cry. Everywhere I look, people are pregnant. Pushing strollers and holding the hands of tiny people, breastfeeding on park benches, eating for two. Everywhere I go women are swelling with life. Just like me.

Every day I can feel myself becoming more and more attached to the unknown, casually rooting myself to the invisible and unthinkable and unimaginable.

I think about all the things I haven't done yet. The novel I haven't finished. The job I haven't secured. And then the little voice inside me says, "But you still can finish that book. You still can secure that job."

But the timing is so terrible. *When is the timing ever right?*

I hadn't planned for this. *Nothing in life is ever planned.*

I'm too young to be a mother. *There is nothing wrong with being young.*

But we have no money! *Plenty of people make it work with far less.*

But no one I know has any children. What if I don't know how to be a mother? *You will figure it out. You are not afraid.*

I don't want to be a housewife. *Great! Then don't be.*

I don't want to have regrets. *You will never regret a decision you make with your heart.*

I don't want to give up everything in my life and just be a mom. *Why do you think you have to?*

I don't want to live life by the book. *You never have before.*

I want to keep this baby. *I know you do.*

Thank you for listening. *Well, duh. . . . I'm your inner voice. It's my job.*

No one knows what to say. I tell my friends. I tell my family. I tell my diary. I know what people are thinking—that if I have the baby I will be giving everything up, leaving my life for the sake of another. I see the looks when I break the news. I know it won't take long before no one calls me. No one wants to party with a pregnant girl. No one wants to tell the young mother his secrets or relationship problems or story ideas. No one wants to lie and talk shit and collaborate on an art installation with a baby crying in the background. And yet for once I don't care what anyone thinks of me.

I feel proud. Empowered by my pregnancy and by a suddenly changed life. So I step onto the edge of the world, and with both hands, throw the slabs of truth like stones and watch the ripples curl and push out into the unknown.

It's your call.

I know I am ready. For me, being ready has always meant not being ready at all. Because when is anyone ever ready for what they do not know? This is the time. This is my body. My instincts. My life. And I have never been able to follow the rules. I have instead forged my signature to humor the lemmings and gone my own way. Dropping out of college to pursue my career, sneaking in through the back doors of life instead of waiting out front. In the past I may have lived life fast. Breaking the speed limit and racing down the freeway with music blasting, ashtray overflowing, all by myself. But I'm ready for a change. I am no longer alone.

"I want to have this baby."

Hal nods, takes me in his arms, and kisses me, and as we combine in one another's tears, I swallow all doubt and choke back the fear, all of the questions, and everything suddenly becomes very clear. I am not on drugs or dreaming. I am pregnant, and soon I will be a mother.

Holy fucking shit.

Life flexes its muscles and I recline against the complexity of the future, kaleidoscopic, ever-changing, brilliant with color and an infinity of diamonds. I check my rearview mirror one last time and merge into the carpool lane, across the double yellow lines.

SOME ONE-BEDROOMS
Are Bigger Than Others

"I GUESS WE SHOULD probably move in together," Hal says.

"Yeah. That seems about right."

"Should we get married?"

"I don't know."

Hal and I are sitting on opposite ends of the patio as he smokes a cigarette. I kick the pavement.

"We don't need to get married, do we?"

"We don't need to do anything."

"Do you want to get married?"

"Not yet. I think moving in together is good enough."

We had talked about moving in together *before*. It was comforting to talk about the future. We would lie side by side after sex, naked and sweaty, and contemplate our future living arrangements.

"How about a big house on a hill overlooking the sea?"

"With seven bedrooms."

"And I'll have a recording space in the guest house out back."

"And my office will be made of windows."

"Whatever you want, baby," he would assure.

Our pillow talk went on like this until one of us would fall asleep—in most cases, Hal. Meanwhile, I'd babble on about devoting an entire mahogany paneled room to my first-edition book collection.

And although the honeymoon period in some of my previous relationships had included talk of moving in together and *I wonder what our babies will look like,* Hal's and my fantasy world has been carefully constructed, an escape for us to crawl toward every night in our dreams. It's less of a risk to build sandcastles away from the sea, so we closed our eyes and followed a paved driveway to a mansion on a cliff with ocean views and an office made entirely of glass. And within its walls, we could be anything we wanted to be. We could pretend we weren't a couple of struggling artists in a city plagued with broken dreams.

Every now and then we'd come back to earth, puncturing our delusions with reality: Moving in together was the practical solution to our financial woes.

"We sleep in the same bed, anyway."

"Why am I paying rent when I'm always here?"

"I know, right? Totally. *Totally.*"

We'd decided to wait until our six-month anniversary to start looking, and we crossed our fingers that by then we'd still be in love.

That was *before*.

We've only been together for five months, but we agree that if we're going to try and have a baby together, we should probably live together first. Hal's current living situation is straddling the line between uncomfortable and very uncomfortable—his bedroom is a converted pantry in the kitchen, where he sleeps with his feet against a tiny window and its broken screen. So naturally, we spend most nights at my apartment. And to make things more complicated, I have two dogs, further narrowing our options.

I sleep with one eye open, laptop on my pillow, refreshing craigslist every five minutes just in case a new listing goes up. We want to make sure we are the first ones on the scene should a really good deal appear at 3:46 AM on a Tuesday. Something local so we don't have to move to the San Fernando Valley. I hate the Valley. I refuse to leave this side of the hill, and Hal doesn't want to move either. If I cannot live in the city, then I will not live near one. I'd rather be haunted by ghosts in old walls than live in a place dead of spirit. A one-bedroom is all we can afford, but some one-bedrooms are bigger than others.

At 3:58 I find a two-bedroom cottage in Silver Lake for $1,750. An amazing deal, even though our ceiling is $1,600. I email the landlord and explain our delicate situation.

Dear Sir,

My boyfriend is a musician, and I'm a writer, and we're going to have a baby. But we love the neighborhood. Your cottage is just perfect for us. Like a dream. Can we make an appointment to see it? Is $1,750 negotiable? We're great people! We pay rent on time.

Yours,

Rebecca Woolf

The landlord emails me back immediately. I'm glad I'm not the only sleepless OCD freak on the refresh key:

Rebecca,

You sound nice. How about you come by tomorrow?

Yours,

Bob

I nudge Hal, who is asleep.

"Wake up! Wake up!"

"I'm sleeping."

"I found the place! This is it!" I shriek.

Hal lifts his head and squints against the light of my iBook. "It's too expensive."

"But I'm in the midst of a negotiation!"

"There's no way that guy's going to go down for you. Look at that place!"

"Of course he will! I am *the* master negotiator."

Hal shakes his head and rolls over. "Fine. We'll go look, but don't get your hopes up."

Too late. I have already decided which window to park my desk against.

The cottage is even more beautiful than in the photos. Tall slanting roof with window boxes and white roses outlining a winding path of pebbles. A birdbath sits outside the window. *Our* window. The door is open and no one is here, so we step in and I gasp. It's so perfect I could cry. I throw myself on the floor and flap around squealing.

"Sold!" I yelp. "We'll take it!"

Hal nudges me with his foot.

"Um."

"Could this be any more perfect?"

"It's pretty nice, but . . . "

"Leave it to me," I interrupt. "I got this one."

The landlord is at the door, knocking. I hadn't realized I locked the door behind me. I'm very comfortable here.

"Sir! Hello! I'm Rebecca! I emailed you. We'll take it! Sixteen hundred, right?"

"Refresh my memory. I got a lot of emails," he says.

"Writer. Pregnant . . . "

"Yes! I remember, now. Congratulations. What do you write?"

"Books. Well, trying to at least."

"Me too!"

I nudge Hal. This guy is going to be no problem to break. I may even be able to get him down to fifteen hundred.

"What are you writing?" I ask him.

"Well," he says. "I just finished a novel about a man who kills people and makes hot dogs out of them, and then he sells them at this restaurant where he works. I'm really into cannibal horror stories. It's just this thing I have. I have a copy in my car if you want to read it."

"I'd love to!"

This time Hal nudges me.

"And by the way, we've thought long and hard about the cottage and . . . we'll take it! For sixteen hundred!"

Bob hands me a folded copy of the lease and tells me we have to apply first. "And the price is seventeen fifty, not sixteen hundred."

"Hmmmm. Are you sure?" I say, patting my cheek with my finger.

"I'm pretty sure," he replies, standing his ground.

"Okay, then. Seventeen-fifty it is."

Hal steps in front of me. "Thanks for the lease. We'll get this back to you later this afternoon."

"But . . . "

"Not a problem," Bob says. "We'll talk soon I hope!"

On our way out the door, we pass two other couples ogling the impeccable garden. "I just hope they wipe their feet outside the door so they don't track dirt into my house," I mumble.

The car is silent on the way home. Hal turns down the music and looks over at me. I flick the volume up and look ahead, watching the road. There is nothing to say. We know what the other one is thinking, so instead of arguing aloud, we do so silently. He thinks I'm being a spoiled asshole, and so do I. We're both right.

I wish I didn't have to be so naive. I wish I could take back all of the frivolous purchases of my past. The $700 Gaultier skirt I had to have and never wore. The $500 dinner tab I "took care of" because I felt insecure around my professionally successful friends.

I'm angry with myself for not being able to afford $150 more a month because of my designer shoe habit. I'm angry with myself for being angry that I have to change. I'm frustrated that daydreams come so naturally that I can trick myself into justifying anything. I'm disappointed that a part of me still believes it's possible for Hal and me to wake up cazillionaires or, at the very least, the luckiest people in history, able to afford to rent our window-filled dream house on a hill in the clouds for $1,595.

I'm angry that we're broke and that we had to get pregnant right now, of all times, when we can barely support ourselves.

"I'm sorry. I know you really wanted the cottage."

"I'm sorry too."

"We need to save money now, you know."

"Yeah."

"Babies aren't cheap."

"I know."

"Don't worry. We'll find a place," Hal smiles.

I smile back. "A cute one?"

"The cutest."

"It's probably just as well," I say. "I was kind of afraid the land-lord was going to kill us and make us into hamburgers."

"It was hot dogs."

"It was weird."

"It was a sign."

"Yeah, maybe it was."

We wrap back down the hill and head west toward Hollywood on roads surprisingly clear of traffic for rush hour on a Friday—a sign perhaps that our dream apartment is still out there. That all we need is to turn a corner and there it will be. *God, I hope so.* I have already explained to my landlord that I will not be renewing my lease, and Hal's pantry has a maximum capacity of one.

We need a cosigner. And help with the deposit. It's embarrassing. We're not supposed to still need our parents, but we do. We look like shit on paper.

"My dad will cosign," I say to Mr. Barry, our new future landlord.

Mr. Barry's a bearded and overweight mama's boy who doesn't

know he's gay. This makes him cranky. He's always with his mother, who follows him around in her beat-up old minivan, slapping movie posters on the wall of the lobbies of the various apartment buildings they own in the neighborhood.

"What does your dad do?"

"He's a physicist."

"Okay. Fair enough. But I'm going to have to talk to him," he insists.

Mr. Barry loves my dad. He keeps repeating how smart he is and how flawless his credit is, insinuating that we're a couple of loser kids squatting on his property thanks to my father, who he seems to believe has saved us from becoming bag people on Skid Row.

I want to feel sorry for Mr. Barry, but I want to punch him in the balls even more. I restrain myself, however, because at this point, we're desperate. The dogs and I will be homeless in two weeks.

"We'll manage," I say, soaping up Hal's back in the shower.

"I just hate that Mr. Barry guy. Did you see the way he looked at me? What a dick."

"But the apartment's cheap. Thirteen fifty for a one-bedroom in that neighborhood is really good."

"I suppose."

I hand Hal the bar of soap and turn around.

"My turn."

We arrive to sign the papers. We have both agreed not to say anything to Barry the Bastard about my pregnancy. I won't be showing
for a while, so it's just going to be our little secret.

"It says here you have pets. What kind?"

"Two dogs."

"Big dogs?"

"One of them is—Cooper, he's a boxer. And then there's Zadie.
She's a Boston terrier."

Mr. Barry sighs and crosses his arms. He shakes his head,
removes his glasses, and wipes at his eyes.

"You didn't tell me anything about big dogs!" he howls. *Someone forgot to take his meds this morning.*

"We're willing to pay a pet deposit," I say. "And they're very
well behaved."

"That's what everyone says about their dogs!" Mr. Barry paces
for a minute while Hal and I kick each other under the table.

"I'm ready to walk," Hal says under his breath. "This guy is nuts."

I tell him to calm down. I want this apartment. I'll do whatever the jerk-off says. I just want to find something and be done
with it.

Mr. Barry breaks from his tantrum and returns to the table.
"You're going to have to get the big dog insured."

"Uh. O . . . kay," I say, masking my confusion with a smile.

"And I'd like you to pay a monthly animal fee that I will add to the price of your rent."

I give Mr. Barry a knowing look. We both know this is illegal. We should be giving the man a pet deposit in case the dogs damage anything. A pet "fee" means we'll never get the money back, and that's not the way it works, *Barry*.

"What kind of fee are we talking about?"

"I'll have to get back to you on that," he says.

An hour later we get a fax with the following:

Big Dog.................................... *$65*
Small Dog................................. *$1*

I have no idea where he came up with these numbers. I wonder what he factored into the equation to come up with one measly dollar for Zadie's monthly rent.

"This dude just gets crazier," Hal says, reluctantly signing his lease. He hands it to me so I can finalize the deal.

"I'm glad we didn't tell him I was pregnant. We might have had to pay a fetus fee."

≥ ⋇ ⋹

Today is my first appointment at the ob-gyn. Hal can't make it because he has to work. He has a new job, so he has to be careful when he calls in sick, but he's promised to take off for the next one.

"Rebecca?" the nurse calls over her shoulder, and I stand up, startled by the sound of my own name. I follow her into the back room. "The doctor will be with you shortly."

I lie down on the bed for several minutes, but no one's coming, and I feel bored and vulnerable lying here. I flip through the stack of magazines in the plastic bin on the wall and come to *Highlights for Children* magazine.

"I love *Highlights for Children!*" And then I remember that this magazine is not for me. It's for a child. *Maybe my child will love* Highlights for Children. I open up the magazine to an animal maze that has already been solved in green Magic Marker.

Somebody's kid, I think.

Seconds later, my new doctor is knocking at the door.

"Rebecca!" he says, like we're old friends.

"Doctor!"

He takes a seat beside me, pulls out his clipboard, and asks me a hundred questions, including:

"Are you married?"

"No."

"Are you planning on getting married before the baby is born?"

"Um. Not sure."

The doctor explains to me the importance of knowing for insurance purposes. He uses words like "custody" and "family," words that scare me because I don't know what to do with them.

I hate paperwork. I hate signing leases and legal documents. I always feel like I'm going to get lost in the fine print and be enslaved between the consonants of words I don't understand.

There is so much paperwork with a new apartment and a new doctor. So much paperwork in a new life. I feel like someone's taking snapshots of me in the dark without a flash. I'm trying as best I can to hold still, to stay in focus.

TRIMESTER,
a Broad

OUR NEW APARTMENT is on Detroit Street and 3rd, one block south of Trader Joe's, a block west of La Brea. I've been living in this area of Los Angeles on and off for five years, since I was eighteen, when I moved from my childhood home in suburban San Diego. It's a cozy neighborhood full of aspiring actors and musicians who practice their singing in the windows of their studios. Marijuana and incense curl from the vents like steam, and nobody knows my name. They will not ask for it either. No one cares. And honestly, neither do I. Everyone is busy concentrating on being ambitious, posing in front of the mirror with flexed muscles, practicing Oscar acceptance speeches and Sundance pick-up lines while phony checks for a million dollars hang above their futons like dreamcatchers. I am no different, except that the million-dollar check I wrote myself is in my underwear drawer, and

I stopped smoking weed and have never had any muscles to flex. I'm no different, except for the fact I have a baby in my body the size of a pumpkin seed.

I might as well be the only pregnant woman in the whole world, because no one around here has kids. Dogs, yes. But no kids. Women grow old and die before they become pregnant here. They adopt cats and take in stray dogs and stray lovers. They show up for auditions, vying with women half their age for the same part. They read the lines and think, *I can be this person. I can be anyone.* They spend their whole lives reaching toward the dream. Skimming the cluttered pond with calloused fingertips.

A part of me is already envious of their freedom. A part of me is envious of my former self for having had that. For being like everyone else: ambitious and optimistic with fingers crossed, believing.

I watch them out the kitchen window. Leaving their apartments. Smoking cigarettes. Flicking their butts into oncoming traffic.

I miss smoking, sitting at my computer with an ashtray and a bottle of Two Buck Chuck, taking drags and blowing them against the screen, faking my own artistic demise, my hand across my forehead for dramatic effect. Even when I smoked alone, I pretended people could see me. I'd exhale smoke out my nose like a dragon and wink at my reflection in the computer screen, so the typed words looked like they were coming out of my eyes.

I feel like an idiot for missing it, for being the stereotypical writer chick and pretending I was a somebody. We're all either somebodies or nobodies, depending on which way we choose to look at it.

⇒ ✲ ⇐

Our bedroom has spores from water damage. It has never rained so much in Southern California as it has these last few weeks, and I keep thinking our apartment is going to wash away, down La Brea toward the 10 Freeway. Because that is what the news keeps saying. Trying to scare me. And it's not fair, because before I didn't care, but now I have someone to be scared for.

When our lease is up, we plan to move into something bigger. The baby will be five months old by then, and we presume that we will be making enough money to afford something twice as expensive. We cross our fingers. We believe.

⇒ ✲ ⇐

Our kitchen table is also our desk, and we eat dinner on our closed laptops and work through the night. Our chairs don't match. Hal's is made out of wood, and mine is an old desk chair missing a screw. And when I lean on the table too hard, the glass flips over and lands on my lap.

Hal has been working as a production assistant for the past few months, which means he gets paid nothing to work fourteen-hour days. Meanwhile, I've taken a job writing for an adult website to pay the bills. I'm not making enough money at my day job, where

I work for a nonprofit as a chat-host for kids with chronic illness. I love the kids too much to leave, so I had to find some other way to supplement my income. My bosses at my porn job still don't know I'm pregnant because I wore a trench coat to the interview. I was afraid I wouldn't get the job if they knew I had a baby on the way. I realize I'm not showing yet, but still. I was afraid my editorial duties would be limited to press releases and staff biographies if they knew the truth. I've lived in Los Angeles long enough to know how to fake it. Fake orgasm. Fake age. Fake not being pregnant.

All I want to eat are baked potatoes stuffed with sour cream and bacon bits. I'm craving meat like the red-blooded animal I am. Bacon bits may not seem hardcore, but to me, anything red is rebellious, especially because the last time I had a slice of bacon I was twelve.

"They're not real bacon bits," Hal says, witnessing my pile of flesh morsels.

"Are you sure?"

"It's facon."

"Then how come it tastes so much like bacon?"

"How would you know what bacon tastes like? When was the last time you ate the real kind?"

"I assumed I was eating it now, but I guess not."

I am disappointed that I'm still a vegetarian. I thought by now

I would have rebelled against my decade of antimeatness in favor of the insatiable joy of the flesh. But as it turns out, I'm still clean. I'd made a conscious decision to eat bacon because I felt like it was something I was supposed to do. Because pregnant people have cravings like pickles on ice cream, and pregnant vegetarians order plates of meat at dinner. Or maybe that is just how they do it in the movies. My mom craved meat with me. She told me that all she ate when she was pregnant was lamb shanks and tenderloin. I don't know what I'm craving besides baked potatoes. Chemicals, I guess. Facon. *Clever bastards.*

"All this time I thought I had become carnivorous."

"Bacon bits do not a carnivore make."

"Whatever."

I pour the ranch dressing on nice and thick all over my potato so it oozes down the sides of the punctured skin.

Oh yeah. Like that.

On my way home from work, I drive through Jack in the Box. I haven't had fast food in five years, but I feel like having a taco. And it's all I can afford with an ashtray overflowing with pennies and nickels. I know that Jack in the Box sells two tacos for ninety-nine cents because there is always a sign on the window that says Two Tacos for 99 Cents! so I decide that's what I will have. Two tacos. Dead cow. Ninety-nine cents.

"The two tacos are made from soy," Hal says, interrupting my feast when he walks through the door.

"What the hell are you talking about? Why would they be made from soy?"

"For the vegans."

"It isn't even advertised as soy! And soy is always more expensive!"

"It's cheap soy. They buy it in bulk."

I don't know who to believe, so I believe no one. Not my boyfriend nor the Internet, which I peruse for the truth and instead find a series of conflicting arguments.

I walk the dogs to the nearest 7-Eleven and buy seven packs of beef jerky.

"Are these made from real beef?"

The man at the counter looks at me with a puzzled expression.

"It says beef jerky, but it isn't really soy jerky, is it? Because I only want it if it's real animal flesh."

He looks over at the woman next to him, who I assume is his wife. She is also pregnant—except unlike me, she is actually showing.

"Never mind," I say, winking at the pregnant woman with the big eyes.

They think I'm crazy. And maybe I am. But this time I will have my beef. My chewy stick of tortured dead cow.

I eat three pieces before I feel nauseated and pledge never to eat meat again. I will have nightmares of cow carcasses for a week.

⇒ ✴ ⇐

"Do I look pregnant yet?" I ask.

"Not yet," Hal responds.

I study myself in the mirror every day, pressing my belly against the glass, examining my shape from all angles. I wonder what it looks like in there. I wonder if it knows that I am watching. I take photos of myself in the mirror as I grow, and they all come out blurry or strange. I save only a few, and the rest I drag into the trash can of my laptop.

⇒ ✴ ⇐

"Do I look pregnant yet?"

"Not yet."

I lie awake at night asking the universe questions. I imagine that I am carrying the North Star. *If ever you are lost, look to the North Star to find your way home.* We learned that in Girl Scouts, along with *Make new friends and keep the old; one is silver and the other gold.*

I think a lot about that. Make new friends and keep the old. The way our little-girl voices sounded in harmony as we sang. The words and what they meant to me then. What they mean to me now. I'm trying to keep old friends, but it's hard.

I have always had a lot of friends, the kind of friends you go out with, who know your name but not your story. The kind of friends who never ask, who cannot be bothered to know. Mutual acquaintances disguised as friends. In one ear and out the other. Friends like one-night stands. *Was I drunk last night? Did we sleep together? Did we talk to each other? Do I know you? I'm sorry, what's your name?*

People are disappearing. My best friends have fallen off the earth. I didn't realize that the sidewalk ended for those who will soon push strollers. I feel like I'm hanging midair. I don't have a place anymore. I'm not one of *them*. But I'm not one of *them*, either. Ask me who *they* are, and I don't even know. People with children. People without.

I am neither.

I am alone.

I erase phone numbers, contacts, friends, men who have drained me financially, emotionally, little lost boys with feathers in their hats and parents who never cared enough to say "I love you."

"But *I* love you," I would say. To every one and all of them, and maybe I did. But only so they would love me back. I loved that my love was enough to make a difference, at least until morning. I loved that my words could be an easy fix. Fix a moment. Fix an hour. Fix a life. I loved that I got to be the strong one.

I opened myself like a shelter, letting the world inside. Up all night to talk a friend off a ledge or away from a needle or her fourth married man. Because taking care of others was how I took care of myself. I thought I was saving the world, one lost boy at a time, but I was killing myself without even realizing it.

I don't want to bring my child into a world where drug addicts might pass out on our doorstep. Or call at 3:00 AM from a pay phone in the Valley.

"I'm here. Can you please pick me up?"

I want everyone out of my life who has taken from me and not given back—all the cool cats living their ninth lives. I do not want them near my child. Not even now, as it grows inside me.

So I screen my calls. I stop answering my phone after midnight. Whatever it is, it can wait. I am not the world's beck-and-call girl. Not anymore.

There are parties, but I'm no longer invited, and when I am, I'd rather not show up. I'm not going to be the pregnant girl in the bar. Or the sober girl at the party. I'm too old for that. Wait, never mind, I'm too young.

"Do I look pregnant yet?"

"Not yet."

When I go out in public, I am conscious of the fact that I look exactly the same but I am now totally different. I convince myself that I can feel the baby kicking even though the Internet tells me the baby is the size of a garbanzo bean. Or an olive. Or a very small strawberry. Or a legume. It is a strange feeling to know I am pregnant when no one else can tell. I go in to work like everything is normal. I say nothing. I am the shy girl who mutters to herself in the corner, but I don't care.

"She's getting fat," they will say until they figure it out. And when they do, they'll feel like idiots for thinking I was fat. And then I will feel relieved that the tipping scale has nothing to do with the baked potatoes. Or the beef jerky. It has to do with something else. *Someone* else.

I'm not here to make friends. I'm here to work. And scribble ideas for baby names when no one's looking.

Completely clueless, and with no friends or family with babies or even children, I decide to do what women do when they get pregnant and have no idea what they're doing. I sign up for week-by-week newsletters and spend a day at the bookstore, on my ass, flipping through books. I watch a red-haired woman pull several from the shelf. She has a list in her hand and is muttering to herself as she plucks large glossy manuals and sticks them under her arm. I memorize the titles in her hand and wait for her to leave to grab the same ones.

1. *What to Expect When You're Expecting.* Even though I wasn't expecting to expect.

2. Dr. Sears's *The Birth Book.* By the looks of his family por-

trait and nine children, it would seem Dr. Sears has been using the same birth control method we have.

3. *Dr. Spock's Baby and Child Care.* You mean the dude from *Star Trek* with the pointy ears?

4. *A Child Is Born.* Ahhhh!! Her vagina looks like it's exploding! Close the book! Quick! CLOSE IT!

At the checkout counter, the bookstore employee winks at me and eyes my belly.

I smile and laugh and shrug.

"Congratulations. Is it you?"

"It *is* me," I say.

"Have a nice day."

"Thank you."

I bring the books home and spread them across my bed. I feel like I have just joined a club and have been handed my literature. I'm looking forward to learning the handshake and uncovering the secret code.

Hal pushes open the bedroom door. "What are you doing in there?"

"Studying."

"For what?"

"The baby."

"Anything good?"

"Not really."

I am amazed at the amount of information about breastfeeding. Turns out, there are hundreds of books on the subject. There are clubs and support groups and hotlines and more clubs. In fact, breastfeeding seems to be the most important part of motherhood.

"It's best for baby."

"Important for bonding."

"Healthier."

"Better."

"Do whatever it takes."

"It is your duty. . . . "

Wait.

It's best for my baby? I need to do whatever it takes? It is my duty?

I close the book. I feel sick. There is almost no chance that I will be able to breastfeed and up until now I was okay with that. I start to sob.

"Are you okay in there?"

"Fine! I'm fine. Just hormones. Please go away. I need a moment. Leave me alone."

Once upon a time I was in high school. It was summertime. Lazy days on the beach. Bonfire parties. Making out on the bluffs. Rocking out to the Cardigans in my convertible. I was sixteen the summer I went from a B cup to an E and my hormones went berserk. I was put on the pill and sent to a shrink, and I wrote a lot of sucky poetry. That was the downside. The upside was that overnight I became some sort of Amazonian freak. I had always wanted boobs when I was flat-chested, and here they were. It was like in the movie *Big*, when the boy wakes up as Tom Hanks, checking out his new, larger penis, like, *Whoa! This thing's awesome!*

That was how I felt. *These things are awesome.*

I spent the summer buying custom-made bikinis and getting felt up. The boys I had been crushing on for years were finally crushing on me. All I had to do to get a free ice pop was show up at the snack shack in my low-cut top. No questions asked. I learned very quickly that having large breasts could get me stuff. A revelation? More like a fact of life.

At our high school we had something called "The Whore List," and every year on the first day of school, the senior girls would post it in the bathrooms. My friends and I had been on it every year, not because we were whores but because we dated the senior boys, and senior boys belonged to senior girls, not to sophomores, and especially not to freshmen.

My junior year, I was christened "Number One Whore," which meant it was the senior girls' mission to make my year hell. I was egged, toilet-papered, pushed on my way to class, and the butt of every nasty locker room rumor. My garage was permanently stained with chocolate syrup, my driveway with explicit words scribbled in chalk.

It wasn't funny. It was embarrassing and upsetting and not how I wanted to spend my year. Instant reputation known by all. *Hi, guys. How you doing?* I kept my head held high as I walked past the older girls and their dirty looks. I pretended I didn't care. I started wearing clothes that covered me up. Turtlenecks and boyfriends' oversize T-shirts. When you have really big breasts, you can't help looking a little bit slutty. It's hard to tame the cleavage, even in a large shirt. And though having large breasts may have gotten me what I wanted over the summer, come school time, I wanted nothing to do with my cleavage. I wanted it gone.

I got used to the names and the pencil drops; I got used to laughing off the rumors. I had "slept with the whole school" before I'd even lost my virginity. I could hardly keep up with myself, the fiction of it all.

I tried not to let it bother me. The looks in the locker room, the eye-rolls, the evil stares from women, the freaky dudes trying to cop a feel. The guys at work. On the street. The beach. I laughed it off, gave the ol' "you wish" look and kept on, hunching my back and crossing my arms in front of my chest.

If sex was power, then how come I felt stripped of it? I went through the next two years hating my body. Hating my breasts. Hiding them even from boyfriends, hands cupped, bra on, lights off. Always off. What once seemed like an answer to prayer turned into an unfortunate curse.

It wasn't until homecoming of my senior year, when the entire visitor side of the football field starting chanting "Nice tits, Queenie," that I decided to do something about it. It was mortifying enough having to wave in my tiara and cape and ride around in a Ford Mustang. I left the game in tears. Angry. Out of control. I had thought about surgery before, but this time I was going to do it.

"You might lose all sensation."

"Whatever."

"You probably won't be able to breastfeed."

"Don't care. Just get them off of me."

I waited until I was eighteen to have breast reduction surgery. It was the most painful six weeks of my life. Then, when I was twenty, I had to have the surgery again. My breasts weren't done growing, apparently. That, or they decided to grow back.

Every night I pray for a son. I am afraid of giving birth to myself, and in my dreams I do. The doctor pulls a small and bloodied Rebecca from between my legs, and I don't want to be held. So the doctors take me away screaming.

I am afraid of the looks my daughter will get if she inherits my breasts. Scared that I might wake up one day to chocolate syrup smeared across the driveway. That she might use her body to get what she wants and find out that she was never really in control, even though she told herself she was. And her friends. And her shrink. I am afraid that at eighteen I will have to hold her hand in the operating room, dress her stitches, understand.

I am afraid that she will push me away when I tell her my story. Because I know I would have done the same with my own mother.

The grass is always greener, of course. Pretty girls want to be taken seriously and smart girls want to be called pretty. Small-chested girls wear push-up bras and the big-breasted wish you would look away.

I do not judge women for wanting to change their bodies and for going to great lengths to do so. At the end of the day, we all want to be comfortable in our skin. We want to be beautiful.

After the surgery I ran faster. Men looked me in the eyes instead of at my chest. Women, too. I wore shirts with buttons. I took off my bra and looked at myself naked in the mirror, hands at my sides. I was no longer consumed with what I could not hide, but instead with what I wanted to reveal.

One cannot censor modern times. It is what's on the inside that counts, but it isn't so simple. Not today and perhaps not ever. Sometimes, blinded by the exterior, we cannot look within. And for me I had no choice but to change.

Today I am faced with the reality of the situation. The fact that most likely I will not be able to breastfeed. And according to the books, this is a bad thing. I am less of a woman because of it. I am less of a mother.

I am shocked to find that there are message boards devoted to slamming women who cannot or choose not to breastfeed. Women like me. Apparently it is a terrible thing for a woman who finds sexual satisfaction in her breasts to feel torn and uncomfortable breastfeeding. I search the archives of the message boards for women who disagree. For mothers who stick up for themselves and say, "Fuck you! It's my body! I can choose not to breastfeed if I damn well please."

But they're not there. Only quotes from "the experts." Whatever the hell that means.

I decide that anyone who is going to make me feel guilty is not somebody I am going to go to for help. Ever. So I make a promise to myself that although I will try to breastfeed, I will not feel bad if I cannot.

All I can do is try.

And then try something else.

And do my best.

And fuck the breastfeeding police.

This is motherhood.

And there are no rules.

I put the books away in the box with Hal's old college music manuals. And the ones that don't fit, I throw in the trash.

"But you should read *something*," my mom says to me over the phone. "Books can be helpful."

But I don't want to read another word. I don't want to know what I should and should not do. I don't want to take notes and come up with a birth plan. I don't want to listen to Dr. Sears or Dr. Spock or Dr. Phil. Because they haven't had breast reductions. Because they aren't twenty-three years old. Because they don't know anything about me. Because they want to help me to do what's right for them. Their patients. Their wives. Their philosophies. And I want to do it my way. What were women doing before the age of self-help books and manuals? What's wrong with just winging it? With going with the gut?

I plop down on the couch with a novel.

"What happened to studying?" Hal asks.

"Do you seriously want to go to Lamaze class and wear a whistle around your neck and a #1 COACH T-shirt?

"No."

"Good, because there's no way I could nurse a plastic baby with a straight face. And anyway, we'd for sure get kicked out for accidentally making fun of everyone."

"Okay, so . . . "

"So . . . I'd rather we just do it ourselves. All of it. The birth and the parenting thing and our family. That's our plan."

"Our plan is not to plan?"

"Exactly."

GLOVE
and Marriage

A HARVARD UNIVERSITY STUDY states that 60 percent of pregnancies in the United States are unplanned, and yet I feel like I'm clearly the only woman younger than forty in the waiting room of my Beverly Hills ob-gyn. Women my mother's age give me the once-over and then return to their various pregnancy and childbirth books.

I browse the magazine piles on the mauve side tables but find no copies of *Highlights for Children*. I pluck up a copy of *Sports Illustrated*, left over from 2004, and wonder who selects to the magazines for doctors' offices, and why they are always for old men. *American Angler Magazine* and *Reader's Digest* and *Golf*.

This is a vagina doctor's waiting room, isn't it? How about some help, here?

Not that the parenting magazines are any better. I try to get excited over essays written by suburban housewives about organization and "how to take ten minutes a day just for you!" and I feel bored by the whole idea of parenthood. Nothing exciting or emotionally engaging. Nothing inspiring.

Bland. Everything is bland. The world of parenting is bland. Safe. *Safety first! Prevent, prevent, prevent! Eat more greens for a smarter fetus! If you sleep with one eye open, your child will be more aware!*

"Is this your first?" a woman asks.

"Yeah."

"Me too, and I'm having twins."

"Wow. Double congrats!"

"How old are you?"

"Twenty-three."

"Unplanned?"

"Yeah."

"Wow. I was in no place to have a baby when I was twenty-three."

How do women always find a way to be condescending, even when they're trying to relate? I nod and look down at *American Angler*. I would rather read about fly-fishing lures than explain myself to a Mystic Tanned failed actress and her twins.

Not long after I start showing, people start touching. Approaching me with clammy hands. Pressing their fingers to my belly without permission. Asking me personal questions. Mi uterus is suddenly su uterus, and that goes for men as well, particularly the man who works at the newsstand down the street.

"Are you having a girl?"

"I don't know yet."

"You're having a baby girl."

"Oh. Okay. Thanks."

"I know it sounds crazy. But I can just tell."

"Okay. Can I buy my magazine now?"

Annoyed, I walk home quickly, muttering to myself about the large population of assholes I never knew existed until recently. They pop up like mushrooms everywhere I go.

What is it about assholes and pregnant women? Is the expanding uterus some kind of magnetic field?

Women cross the street to make conversation with me, and men wink at me in elevators. I feel like I am attached to a sign that says "Tell me what you think of my pregnancy! Torture me with your unsolicited advice!"

I come home to a large package on our doorstep. I kick it into the house. It's a heavy box, and I don't recall ordering anything online. I tear it open and pluck out a crisp white card and a box wrapped in matte wrapping paper, stark white with luxe green ribbon.

It's fancy. There is no way I accidentally ordered something and had it gift-wrapped. Especially not a . . .

Mother-of-pearl picture frame?

"What the hell is this?"

I tear open the card and read the following:

Dear Hal and Rebecca,

Congratulations on your nuptials. We wish you the best of luck in your life together as man and wife. Mazel Tov!

Love,

Sarah and Harry Getz

At first I think it's just a mistake. I don't know a Sarah Getz. Perhaps they are friends of Hal's. Maybe it's just a joke.

Ahahahaha! That was a good one!

Then the doorbell rings.

I press my face against the peephole.

"UPS!"

I sign for the package and lock the front door behind me.

"What the . . . ?"

Sure enough, another white box. This time with a sterling silver dessert plate and matching serving spoon inside.

To the Happy Couple!

Mazel Tov on your wedding, and we hear there's a baby on the way! We love you!

Sincerely,

The Rosenbaums

"Who the hell are these people?" I say aloud.

Hal comes home from work to find me making ducks out of wedding-bell wrap.

"Here," I say, passing him the cards.

"What is this?"

"I have no idea! We're getting wedding presents."

"From who?"

"Did I miss something? Did we get married in my sleep?"

Hal is as shocked as I am.

"I don't even know who these people are."

"Well, we have to do something! What are we supposed to do with all these wedding gifts? What am *I* supposed to do? Write a thank-you note and play dumb?"

"I'll call my parents tomorrow," Hal says. "Maybe there was a misunderstanding."

But there wasn't a misunderstanding. Hal calls his mother, and she confesses to the wedding lie before he even asks.

"I told my friends you got married," she says. "You're going to anyway, so I just mentioned to some people that you already did."

"Mom! What? Why? Are you serious?"

"It's no big deal! Just play along with it. I wanted to tell everyone about the baby, but I couldn't unless you were married first. So now everyone thinks you're married and, well, you *know* how everyone can be! They all want to wish you the best and send gifts!"

"But we don't even know if we're getting married."

"No one has to know! It's no big deal," she says.

I pull away from the receiver, where I've been listening to his mother's bizarre rationale. I'm shaking my head but I'm not angry. *How strange.* And then I start to think that maybe she's right. Maybe we *should* get married, buy ourselves a couple of rings and elope. Because I can't think of a good reason why we shouldn't. Especially now that half of the family assumes we already are.

Hal hangs up the phone. "Unbelievable, right?"

"Yeah, unbelievable," I say.

We lie side by side as Hal goes on about household items we don't need and whether or not we should return the gifts and buy some new silverware because we only have one fork, three spoons, and a knife right now and it's hard to eat pasta without a fork.

"Let's just do it," I finally say, half listening to his monologue about how last week he got lost in Bed Bath & Beyond and how hard it is to find anything there besides pillows and candles.

"Do what? Get new silverware?"

"No. Let's just get married."

"Seriously?"

"Why not? We'll go to Vegas for the night. No one has to be there. That way it's just done and we don't have to worry about paperwork at the hospital and we can write stuff off and let's just do it."

I never imagined I would propose marriage to anyone, and certainly not in this way. Then again, I never imagined any of this, and what the hell? What's a wedding anyway? It would sure make things less complicated, and our families would be relieved. Plus, I could use a road trip right about now.

"Do you really want to marry me?"

"Yeah."

"Okay. Let's do it."

"Really? You want to?"

"Why not? I love you."

"I love you too."

"Great."

"Okay, then."

"Okay!"

Hal smiles and kisses my belly, making his way down, down, *down*. . . .

The speedometer reads 85, and I turn up the radio and watch the world bend under the sun out the window of Hal's Honda Civic. So this is it, I guess. Here we are. A shotgun wedding in Las Vegas. Just the two of us and my thirty-week bulge.

I was never one of those girls who imagined her wedding day. I never fantasized about the white gown, the bridesmaids, the "You may kiss the bride." I never cried over the idea that one day my father would give me away. Or dance with me to some cheesy song about butterfly kisses. I never wanted any of that. In fact, a wedding was always my idea of hell.

Maybe because I have never fully believed in marriage. The pressure to love one person for the rest of your life. To be faithful. To take the last name of a family different from your own. But here we are, doing all of it. Except without the white dress. And the bridesmaids. And our parents. And that butterfly kisses song that makes me want to kill myself.

I am hardly a blushing bride. A perspiring bride, yes. My eyebrows need waxing. My roots are growing in a weird shade of ash blonde. My chin is covered in blackheads. My belly is sticking out over my unbuttoned jeans.

"I think I'm going to keep my last name," I say.

"Oh."

"Do you mind?"

"I guess not."

I can't tell if he's lying or not. We've only been together for ten months. We haven't had the last-name conversation yet, and maybe this is a bad time to be discussing it. Then again, we're on our way to get married so I don't know when a better time would be.

"It's just that I like my name. And I like yours too, but it isn't mine, you know?"

⤳ ✲ ⤲

I'm sitting here on the food-stained seats of my future husband's car and I don't even know him, and for some reason that doesn't scare me. I think maybe it should so I ask myself over and over,

Are you sure you want to do this? Because it's all happening really fast. And I nod my head and say *Yes.* Because I want to do this. Because I love him.

Then again, it might just be hormones.

The limo calls up to our suite at the MGM Grand. I'm in the bathroom, and Hal knocks on the door.

"I'll be right there," I say.

Our wedding bands are in the pocket of Hal's pants. My wedding band has Hal's name engraved inside, and his ring has mine. It only cost us $12 extra on eweddingbands.com. I'm wearing a new shirt for the occasion. An off-white Diane Von Fursterberg maternity blouse with paisley flowers. It was a gift from my mother, and last minute I decided it would be nice to wear at our wedding. Except I couldn't find shoes to match, so I had to settle on a pair of purple suede ones with buckles. They're flat and comfortable. My mom bought them for me too.

The limo came with Wedding Package C. Along with a few photographs and a bouquet with five roses. There was a cheaper bouquet with three roses, but it was far too depressing. $10 for a nicer bouquet was worth it to me. Then again, I have a tendency to splurge. We ordered it all online: $199, not including tax.

We hold hands in the back of the limo, and I pretend like I'm not nervous. I crack jokes and make friends with our driver,

Tyrone, who tries to sell us on the idea that moving to Las Vegas would be good for our unborn child.

"Las Vegas is the fastest-growing city in America. A great place to raise children."

"Mmmmhmmmm."

Tyrone doesn't shut up, but it doesn't matter because I'm not listening to him. My brain is screaming at me. My thoughts are wild and contradictory and nervous. There's a Belle and Sebastian song that goes: You know my wandering days are over / Well does it mean that I'm getting boring / You tell me?

And I can't help but sing the words over and over in my head. What if I want to wander? What if I become boring? I am already, aren't I? I've become boring.

You know my wandering days are over.

Getting married is scary. I don't care which way you go about doing it—a fancy wedding with all the trimmings, or a shotgun ceremony in Vegas with no family or friends to watch you. My heart is in my throat. *You know my wandering days are over . . .*

When we arrive at the Little White Chapel and get in line with the other lovers, I realize that I have forgotten our marriage license. We are fifteen minutes from our hotel and already three minutes late for our wedding, and I have managed to fuck up my one responsibility.

The lady at the front desk shakes her head and tells us to come back tomorrow, but tomorrow we will be leaving, first thing in the morning, because Hal has to work. Because we could only afford one night at a nice hotel, and the MGM Grand isn't even that nice.

I feel like I'm going to throw up. I can't even remember a simple piece of paper, so how am I going to remember to be a good mother, a decent wife? A person no longer independent and selfish? How will I learn to leave my head for long enough to take care of my family? To remember important papers? I start to hyperventilate.

"But I'm pregnant," I say, pointing to my belly. "Please?"

A little old woman in a Jesus brooch appears from the shadows and takes my hand.

"Don't worry, dear. We'll marry you tonight. Tyrone will take you back to your hotel, and you can grab your paperwork and come right back."

So we do.

I feel like an asshole for being so out of my head. On the other hand, brides usually have maids of honor and wedding planners and people who know to remember this stuff. And getting married is scary. I don't care what anybody says.

I wonder if Hal can tell that I'm nervous. My armpits are pouring sweat. *Wet T-shirt contest in the Little White Chapel, anyone?* It seems I'm the only one who signed up.

We get back in line, and Hal makes friends with the little old Jesus lady.

"You know, Britney Spears was married here. And Frank Sinatra."

"I know! One of the reasons we chose this place. We checked the website."

"And Bruce Willis and Demi Moore. And Mickey Rooney has been married here twice!"

"So our odds are good!"

"Indeed!" The little old lady seems to have missed the fact that every famous couple she listed has since been divorced.

"Would you like to be our witness?" we ask her.

She nods her head yes.

And so the three of us file into a tiny room with no windows, surrounded by faux flowers and wet paint, and Hal and I exchange vows over the loud blast of *Ave Maria* on the radio/tape deck/alarm clock on the foldout table beside Bob, our minister/receptionist.

Hal takes my hand and we laugh through the entire service.

" . . . and by the state of Nevada I now pronounce you Man and Wife. You may kiss the bride."

We make out.

Bob presses pause on the stereo, cuing the song up for the next happy couple, and Mrs. Jesusbrooch claps and hobbles back out into the fluorescent glow of the chapel office.

Hal and I blink at each other.

"So now what do we do?"

"Be married, I guess."

"Cool. Let's eat."

Twelve hours later, we're back in the car, on our way home to Los Angeles.

"I understand if you want to keep your last name," he says.

"Thanks. I guess I just don't want to replace what has always been me with what has always been you. I feel like I would be in your shadow or something."

The minute the words come out of my mouth, I wonder if it's selfish of me to reject a zillion years of tradition because I want to maintain part of my independence. I wonder how the baby will feel about his mother having her own name.

The truth is, I don't want to have to change. I just hope that doesn't mean something bad.

IT'S NOT ABOUT
the Journey, but the Perspiration

IT FEELS A LITTLE LIKE I just turned sixteen and got my license but have no car. Not that I would know. When I turned sixteen, my parents gave me a white Cabriolet convertible with cow-print seat covers and a CD stereo that flipped open when you turned the car on. It was a surprise. I couldn't stop crying.

I'm not crying now, just staring into space. Nothing's wrong. Everything just feels so . . . normal.

"Now what?" I think.

We went to Vegas to make me an honest woman, but now that I'm back, I feel like a liar, a total fake.

The gifts continue to arrive on the doorstep as I hold the dogs back from the UPS guy who now knows me by name. We have nowhere to put all of this stuff, dishes and vases and picture frames.

And even though we're officially married now, I feel like nothing has changed. I feel like I should look married, or sound married, but everyone is the same, and our house is exactly the way it looked when we left it, and my breakfast is still in the microwave from two days ago when I guess I forgot to take it out.

We are legally wed but I feel like maybe it was just a dream. Maybe I did get married in my sleep.

The week before I found out I was pregnant, I painted a picture of a naked woman with a man coming out of her belly. I glued keys to each of their necks as necklaces and painted locks on their pink hearts. I gave it to Hal, a gift of mammoth proportions.

"It's supposed to be us," I told him.

"Oh. Okay. It's great. Thanks."

It was obvious he wasn't a fan of its hugeness, or the fact that in the painting he looks like someone from Blue Man Group, or that it looks oddly like he is being birthed by a naked woman who doesn't look much like me either. Regardless, the painting hangs above our bed, a sign of some sort. Boy coming out from my belly button. Unborn child. I have felt all these months that I must be having a boy. Otherwise, why did I paint one before I knew I was pregnant? How would I have known?

"It's a girl. You're having a little girl," my mother says.

"I know it's a girl," my psychic aunt tells me. She knew I was pregnant before I did. The day before I took my pregnancy test, she whispered in my ear that I was going to have a baby.

"Now?" I said.

"Maybe. A baby girl. Someday," she said.

Okay, so maybe it wasn't psychic for her to tell me I was going to have a baby . . . someday. But her vague prediction was the reason I took the pregnancy test. And well . . .

In case of a girl, we have picked out the name Colette, after one of my favorite authors and wild women of twentieth-century France. Indeed, she was the original Girl Gone Wild, flashing her ta-tas in the streets on a dare she gave herself, which is one of the reasons I've always loved her. Promiscuous French free spirits with cocked pens and erotica in their oeuvre have always been my greatest heroes. I don't tell Hal the part about the tit-flashing because I don't think he would be pleased. Then again, he suggested the name Cinnamon.

My doctor doesn't like giving ultrasounds. He has sent me for two, but the first one, at eight weeks, was too soon to tell the sex. I had my second sonogram at four months, but the baby was facing the wrong way. My next and final ultrasound will be at my eight-month appointment, but I can't wait that long to know.

"Why don't we just wait until the baby's born and let it be a surprise?" Hal asks.

Oh, I don't know. Maybe because I want to feel like I know what's going on for once? Because knowing whether I'm having a boy or a girl means knowing something. And with so many surprises already, I need that. To know.

"Hell no. I want to know. *Now.* I have to know. *Now!*"

I bring my psychic aunt and my mother with me to the Ultrasound Store in a strip mall, where I have booked an appointment to determine the truth. We wait together in the lobby, thumbing through binders of three-dimensional ultrasound photographs that look like yellowed, mummified rock people.

The technician calls my name, and we file one by one into a giant room full of fake ferns and discount aisle fountains. New Age music pumps from the rock speakers. Glade-scented candles line the wall in room-freshening seance.

I lie down on the plush bedding, old towels, and crepe paper, and wait. The technician lubes me up and presses her wand to my gut. I squeeze my mother's hand.

"Is it a girl?" my aunt asks.

Is it a boy? I ask myself.

"Is it a monkeysquirrel?" I say aloud.

"No," the technician says. "It's a boy!"

She points to my baby's balls on the monitor. "And this, right here, is the penis!"

"His penis is huge!" my aunt cries out.

And I start to cry. Not because of his penis size or my aunt's embarrassing declaration, but because I'm having a little boy. Because I had a feeling. Because I have always wanted to have a son. Because I'm going to be a mother. Because I'm going to have a boy!

"Does he have a name?" the technician asks.

"Archer Sage."

And he's going to be strong and wise and perfect.

Three months to go and I'm taking advantage of my last days of independence. Counting down until I split down the middle, divided in two. I putt around the city and spend air-conditioned afternoons at the Los Angeles County Museum of Art or the Beverly Center Mall or at my desk working. I rub my belly for good luck and write through the night. I meet my friends for coffee, strutting down the street in knee-high boots even though I can't control my balance. I high-five friends with my swelling fingers and barely notice my rings, lost in their folds. I waddle down to the newsstand to collect my weekly trashy magazines.

"It's a boy, by the way," I shout over the honk of traffic and Metro bus engines and exhaust.

The newsstand guy stops stocking and turns. "No way," he says.

"Yes way. I have a photograph of his penis. Shall I show you?"

"Nah."

"Are you sure?"

"I still think you're having a girl."

"Of course you do."

"Have a nice day."

I spend my nights thinking about Archer, the little boy moving inside of me, trapped in the only world he knows. I write him letters about how in two months he will be stretching his legs and touching strange faces, opening his eyes to a new world, seeing the doctors, his father, and finally me.

I cannot imagine what he will say to himself when he sees us for the first time. Everything a vulnerable, soft-skinned first impression. I pat my belly and draw circles where I think his head rests, like a halo round and round. I wonder what he is thinking about. How can he bear to lie awake, curled in a ball, walled in by humidity and darkness, blinking against the occasional beam of light through my belly button? Will he be claustrophobic like me? Will he feel the need to burn holes in the sky, to climb out of a world that at times seems so low to the ground? I ask him questions aloud:

"How are you coping with your own growth? Do you recognize my voice? Your father's? *Just a city booooooy. Born and raised on Souuuuuth Detroiiiit Streeet* . . . I hope you're not pissed at us for singing Journey to you. It's nothing personal."

When people ask me for his name, I tell them, introducing my belly with pride. "Archer. This is Archer."

I know that everything is about to change, that he will escape my body violently and enter a world that Hal and I are wary of.

I hope you will remind me to send you looking for your own hiding places and mountaintops, rather than mapping them out for you. I realize that one day you will find the way without me, so long as I pack you lunch and an umbrella. "Just in case it rains," I will say, and you will roll your eyes most likely and tighten the laces in your boots.

I place the love letters individually in envelopes in my top drawer so that one day he can open them. Maybe when he turns sixteen. Maybe when he becomes a father. I haven't decided yet.

The doctor's office is always full. Standing room only. I'm too pregnant to stand and too nice to say anything to the half-dozen women who don't bother to offer the most visibly pregnant woman in the waiting room a seat. *The least you can do is scoot over, lady.* I sprawl on the floor with the kids and wait for my name to be called.

When I first started coming here, I didn't believe it was possible for me to look pregnant. It was difficult for me to picture myself with a bulging belly and swollen ankles. I look around the room and wonder if the other women are looking at me in the same way: "Am I going to look like *that?*"

"Rebecca?"

I climb to my feet with much effort and stumble down the hall behind the nurse toward the scale.

The nurse double-takes when she weighs me.

"Hmmmm. . . . Looks like you've gained forty-two pounds in two weeks."

"Forty-two pounds? Impossible. It has to be impossible!"

"Yeah, well. It isn't. Jesus, what have you been eating?"

She thinks this is funny, but it isn't. It's mean. I burst into tears and feel like a failure. Like I must have accidentally swallowed 650 cakes or chugged buckets of lard and forgotten.

"What the fuck, man?"

"Oh, honey! It's okay," she says, which makes me want to smack the bitch upside the face.

"Honey? *Honey?*"

There is no way the nurse is older than twenty, and she's calling me *honey?* Pul-ease. *I'm your elder, thankyouverymuch.*

"I've got two kids, so trust me, I know the feeling."

"You have two kids?"

"Mm-hm. A boy and a girl."

Well at least I'm not the only young mom in Los Angeles.

Either I have failed to notice that I have suddenly become morbidly obese or I have been in serious denial. Come to think of it, none of my maternity clothes fit me anymore, but I figured it was just part of the deal.

I am diagnosed with preeclampsia and prescribed bed rest and daily monitoring at Cedars-Sinai. I burst into tears because I don't know what that means. I have never even heard of preeclampsia, so now, on top of feeling hideously disfigured, I feel afraid. For Archer, and for me, and of the next six weeks of sitting on my ass, plucking dog hairs off the couch.

"This wasn't supposed to happen," I say.

But the thing is, it happens. A lot. Complications are common, even for a woman in her prime baby-making years.

I take slow walks up and down the halls of our apartment building, with my hands on my back. Slowly, back and forth, until my feet are raw and bleeding from rubbing the plastic strips between the toes of my flip-flops.

I bump into walls, forgetting that I have almost doubled in size. I hate the way I look, and I hate even more that it matters. I'm home to a human, my baby, and yet all I can think about are the skinny jeans I will never wear again. My pre-pregnancy wardrobe is still boxed up in the back of my closet and XL maternitywear hangs in its place, stained with olive oil splatters from spilling on myself during dinner on the sofa, the only place I'm comfortable.

I should be carted off in a giant crane and taken away to a Coney Island freak show. I don't even look human. My eyes have lost their shape. I cannot look in the mirror to do my makeup so I close my eyes and guess where the mascara goes. My nose has somehow managed to grow across my entire face, and I can barely walk without breathing into a paper bag.

I hate how everyone keeps telling me I look beautiful. They're all a bunch of liars. Some women do look beautiful pregnant. But I look like Santa Claus without a beard, and Santa Claus without a beard isn't beautiful.

When a guy hits on me in the elevator on my way to my daily monitoring session, I want to have sex with him right then and there. I can't believe he would even think to court a woman with a face resembling an elephant's ass.

I thank him, tell him I'm married, but I would like to get his number just in case. *You never do know.*

Rather than waiting for me to contract naturally, my doctor books an appointment for my induction at 10:00 PM on May 22, four days before my due date. I'm relieved, even though I have been told via "birth plan message boards" to resist induction. To resist doctors and drugs and hospital births.

I want to have this baby as soon as possible. That's *my* birth plan. And I'm not going to fight The Man on this one. Nope. In this case, The Man is my friend.

The days are forever. I feel like I've been sitting on the couch for my entire life, swelling up like an allergic reaction. I cannot see my feet when I stand, even if I try to bend over. I wake up to hair on my pillow and piss in my pants. Because I cannot control my body, it no longer belongs to me. Because sex has become more of a challenge than a fulfillment and my "pussy" is now a "vagina." And pretty soon a person is going to come out of it. *My pussy*. Except I can't call it a pussy anymore. And I have a sneaking suspicion that "cunt" is off-limits too.

I stare up at the naked woman in the painting. She was supposed to be me, except now I don't recognize her: flat-bellied and bare-breasted with short hair. My body has changed so much. My body will change so much more.

Archer's moves become rapid, and I turn on my back so Hal can press his ear to the stretching shell and hear the ocean. So that he can trace the movements with his fingers and feel an entire world underwater. And he looks up at me, still resting on the conch of questions, and we feel the baby's movements together. Three sets of hands exploring my body, motivated by life's natural impetus, the forces that be.

And we lie together through the night and wait.

CHILDBIRTH ISN'T
for Pussies, It's for Vaginas

*

MY PUSSY IS ABOUT TO become a vagina. My tits are about to become breasts. I am well aware of this fact and unable to think of anything else. I am not afraid of the pain of childbirth. Or whether or not I'll be able to handle being a parent. I'm afraid for my sexuality. What if I tear, or the doctor, cutting the slit between my legs, estranges me from my sex? I'm worried that my sexual self will die the moment Archer is born. That my sensuality will become a mere memory, tomorrow's missing piece.

I fear for the life of the soft spot between my legs, which up until now has been in relatively good shape. I fear for her tightness. Her youth. I am terrified that what was once a clean-shaven porn-star-esque pussy will now become a bushy vagina that hangs low like a wizard's sleeve. I'm petrified that having sex is going to be like throwing a hot dog down a hallway, that men will soon think of me as a mother with a baby's bloody head poking out between her legs instead of someone they want to have sex with. I don't want to be perceived as a baby-making machine instead of a sex object; I don't want to lose my feminine power—a power that, no matter how hard my friends try to deny it, is based on sex.

When I first confessed to my mother that I was pregnant, she sighed and said, "I'm just glad that it didn't happen sooner."

"Mom!"

It was her sweet way of calling me a slut because I enjoyed sex with men I loved and strangers I didn't. I liked feeling good. I took advantage of being single and sexual. I said "Yes" a lot.

"Childbirth is a beautiful thing," she said. "You'll see. And you'll finally understand the way I love you. You'll feel my pain."

Childbirth has always freaked me out. From the moment I learned the truth about sex and reproduction, I couldn't look at a pregnant woman without thinking about her legs over her head, pushing a baby out of her vagina. One would think I would have grown out of such thoughts, but quite the contrary. I am still overcome by vivid images of childbirth when I hear the word "mom."

Fifth-grade sex education was a rite of passage for ten-year-olds the community over, an enlightening and petrifying experience. In retrospect, sex ed was about as ridiculous as the D.A.R.E. to keep kids off drugs program. Contrary to what the board of dumbasses had intended with such programs, D.A.R.E. made drugs seem cool, while sex ed made sex seem like cruel and unusual punishment.

I was a fairly sheltered child and clueless about sex. I knew that "it" happened but never spent much time figuring out when and how. I was shy, a late bloomer whose role model was a flat-chested doll that smelled like strawberries. I had a friend a couple of years older who had already endured sex ed and liked to brag about it to me and my friends, quizzing us and getting blank stares in return.

"Rebecca? Do you know what a condom is?"

"Um, yeah. Who doesn't? Psh."

"Oh reaaaaaallly. Draw me a picture, then."

I searched the archives of my brain for clues before remembering the scene in *Naked Gun 2-1/2* where Leslie Nielson and Priscilla Presley dress like plastic gloves and make out. Yes, I distinctively remember them using the words "protection" and "condoms," so I drew something that looked like this:

I believe her exact words were: "What the fuck?"

I wish I could have answered her, but "fuck" was a relatively new word in my vocabulary, so once again I found myself staring blankly as the bitch rolled her eyes and scribbled over my drawing.

"A condom looks like this," she said, drawing a simple circle. "Get it straight. And speaking of straight, once you put it on someone's penis, it looks like this:"

"I knew that," I retorted. "I was just making sure that *you* did."

Sex education was an inevitable fifth-grade experience. Every day drew closer to the moment of truth. Kind of like death. When it was finally announced that we would be having sex ed the following day, I felt relieved. The suspense was giving me an ulcer.

My teacher, Ms. Jackson, separated the Jimmy Z/Gotcha–wearing boys from the Keds- and Hypercolor-clad girls, the mullets from the bangs. She led the Mikes, Chrises, and Brians out of the classroom to the room next door to watch penis videos with the man-teacher so we could watch our "period pieces" with Ms. Jackson.

Oh sweet Moses! Help me, please!

I was already suicidal.

Luckily for us, Ms. Jackson didn't talk much. She drew a picture of a cow and called it the "female reproductive system." She then asked one of the eight Amandas in our class to flip the switch as we all crowded onto the carpet to watch Mickey Mouse point out the clitoris. Minnie Mouse must have been sick the day of shooting.

I was appalled. What the hell was Mickey doing with a pair of ovaries and a box of Tampax? Was it possible for Pluto to contract genital warts? And why was Donald suddenly performing a pap smear? There wasn't a dry eye in the house. Scarred for life, we huddled together like penguins and waited for the storm to end.

"Amanda G., lights up, please?"

Silence.

"Does anyone have any questions?"

More silence.

"Good, because we have another movie to watch. It's called *A Child Is Born*, and it's a beautiful film about the miracle of childbirth! Something you all have to look forward to . . . "

Gulp.

"Amanda Y., lights down, please."

It had become Pavlovian. Lights down = high fever and acute case of asthma. I wanted to be excused to go to the nurse's office, but it was too late. The film had begun. I don't remember much about the movie besides an obscene amount of pubic hair, saggy breasts, and a bloody carcass. If this was what womanhood was all about, I would have to stay a child. Puberty? I would fight it with a razor. No hair here. No way. And the bloody carcass? Weren't periods violent crime enough? The film ended a hundred years later, and as Amanda Q. flipped the light switch, I crawled out from under my desk to politely raise my hand.

"Does it always look like that?"

"Childbirth can be messy, but it is a miracle," Ms. Jackson gushed. "The miracle of life! Just like that tiny newborn, you also came into the world the very same way, through the birth canal and out of your mother's vagina."

Errrrrrrrrrt. Check, please.

It took me a few days before I could look my own mother in the eye. I was fasting as well, and speaking only in code. In my dreams Mickey Mouse was rowing a hairy canoe down the fallopian tube singing *Zipppppety doooo daaaah!* Not cool at all.

About a week later, after the rubble had settled and I was almost able to properly pronounce vowels, Ms. Jackson explained joyfully that it was time for round two of sex education. "But today you will be learning about the boy's reproductive system and the workings of the penis!"

"Penis" was always a lot easier to hear and say than "vagina." "Penis" sounded cool, and "vagina" sounded exactly how it looked. I could handle studying the penis. It was easy to draw and understand. It was straightforward and seemed easy to use. Vaginas, on the other hand, were complex, like black holes of doom.

Amanda R. flipped the switch, and we all took our places on the carpet. The movie started, and with it came the same Mickey Mouse and gang with their pointing sticks and songs about glans and semen. Most of it seemed to be about masturbation and nocturnal emissions.

"One day you will experience a wet dream, Mouseketeers! Now, don't be alarmed! It's perfectly natural."

Of course, when the lights went up, every girl in the class had a raised hand. The little girls of Ms. Jackson's fifth-grade class seemed to be more interested in the workings of the penis than they were of their own genitalia. In the future, this would make a lot of sense.

As for me? I was busy taking notes so I could educate the younger neighborhood girls to save them the shock and humiliation of it all.

It's funny how things change. How one day I went from being scared of boys to turned on by them. How sex went from disgusting and *I can't believe my parents ever did THAT* to *Amazing* and *I can't get enough*.

I wake up suddenly. My heart is pounding. I can't breathe. In my dream my vagina was dragging behind me like a train, and I was trying to tuck it between my legs, petrified that someone would notice.

I feel for my crotch to make sure I haven't suddenly become a gaping hole with a face and feet. I stagger toward the bathroom and crouch over the toilet and try to hold myself back in place.

Every day I do Kegels for hours at a time. No one can tell, but I'm squeezing the daylights out of nothing, trying to seal the hole shut—or at the very least, keep it neat and tight and orderly. Because I want to feel good—like a virgin, touched for the very first time.

I find myself asking questions. To myself and to the clouds that look like breasts dancing across the sky. *Not tits: breasts*.

* Do women love sex because we would make great mothers?
* Is our wanting to orgasm more or less the same as needing to give birth?
* Do *I* love sex because *I* am meant to be a mother?
* What is the relationship between being sexual and being motherly?
* Is a woman merely a man with a womb?

I have no idea what the answers are. I do know that all these years of masturbating and bleeding and *craving cock* have nothing to do with me being sexually alive. It is, simply put, a biological instinct. To make babies. To be a mother. Suddenly I don't feel so powerful. Or sexually liberated. Or naughty. I feel mammalian. Perfunctory.

The doctor stretches a latex glove over his hand and slides it inside me, pressing on my cervix to see how dilated I am.

"This may pinch a little."

"Okay."

"This is going to feel like a lot of pressure, okay?"

"Yeah."

And suddenly a man's hand is inside my vagina. And there is nothing sexual about it. And I am on my back with my legs spread apart not because I want to fuck, but because I'm about to be invaded by cold tools and measuring objects.

And I feel like a child again. Like a little girl, except instead of being afraid of my sexuality, I am afraid it will go away.

The car seat in the back seat is empty on our way to the hospital. Very empty. It is all I can look at as we drive away in silence. Excited. Scared. My teeth start chattering like they do when I'm cold, except I'm not cold at all. I'm sweating.

I touch my belly. *How is it possible that what's in here will soon sit back there?* I ask myself, pushing on my stomach where I can feel Archer's heel pressing against me like a nudge.

We wait in the triage for my doctor. I fill out the paperwork, watching a woman's water break on the floor by my feet. *Oh my god,* I think. *That's going to happen to me.*

The doctors induce me at 11:00 PM. They hook me up to the Pitocin and leave us alone. Hal busts out his camera and starts filming me. I can't imagine how terrible I look. I am well aware that the camera adds twenty pounds, which would make me, in my present state, 222 pounds. Not exactly a screen siren. More like a fire truck.

Hal unpacks his backpack and opens *America,* by John Stewart. He starts reading to me to pass the time, but it hurts when I laugh. So he stops and turns his camera back on to interview the nursing staff.

I watch the clock. Nothing is happening, but it will soon. Still, I can't wait. The suspense is nauseating. I'm ready to meet my baby.

I'm ready to see my feet. I'm ready to not be bedridden for a month. I want a drink. A glass of wine. Or smoke a cigarette. *God, I could use a cigarette right now.*

We wait for hours. Hal drifts in and out of sleep on the plastic couch beside my bed, and I watch the Pitocin drip, and the monitor, and I knock on my belly.

"Hello? Archer? Are you ready or what, little dude?"

But he doesn't answer back. It is nearly 7:00 AM, and nothing. I'm not even in pain. I don't feel a thing. A part of me believes that my pain threshold is superhuman. My contractions are on top of each other, and still I feel nothing. Boredom can be worse than agonizing pain, or so I think. I am beginning to fear the baby will never show his face. I start to whine.

A med student who can't be older than me knocks twice and then pushes through the doors to our room. He introduces himself and shakes my hand, which is ice cold. It's freezing in here. He stretches a latex glove over his hand.

Gulp.

"I am here to check your progress," he says, which apparently is medical speak for "I'm here to fist you for two minutes." He manages to strike up a conversation with Hal about the Yankees. One hand inside me, the other high-fiving my husband for knowing his baseball stats.

Oh my god, I think. *It's happening already. My own husband doesn't even notice that some dude is fisting me.* Because some dude *isn't* fisting me. He's just pressing on my cervix to see how dilated I am.

"Two centimeters still," he announces. "You haven't changed since you arrived."

Oh. Great news, thanks. Look forward to you entering my vagina with metal tools soon. Next time please bring me a Push Pop.

Somewhere between four and six in the morning, shit starts to hurt, but instead of complaining, I choose to buck up and take it like a cave person. If women of the Mesozoic era could handle this, then so can I. I forget one small fact, however: Women of the Mesozoic period did not have Aleve for headaches and Midol for cramps (not to mention there *were* no women during the Mesozoic era, but that isn't my point). Our threshold for pain is not what it used to be, at least not in the Western world. Not when there is a purple pill for every pain and every emotion that isn't quite right or normal. It doesn't take me long to realize that cave woman I am not.

I ring the nurse bell. *I need an epidural on the double, people. Now.* Except it doesn't quite work that way.

"It's a busy night," the nurse explains. "There are four or five women ahead of you."

I imagine it's because Cedars-Sinai is such a Hollywood hot spot, and there's probably a line out the door of pregnant starlets seeking pain relief.

"Fine," I say, because I have no choice. "I'll wait."

Meanwhile, Hal pushes his camera in every nurse's face,

zooming in on every wall and metal tool and the empty plastic bassinet beside my birthing bed. Our baby will soon be out of my body, into the world, twitching and moaning in that plastic thing, which is weird to think about. Fortunately or unfortunately, I can't think of anything right now. Only the pain.

I am relieved when I see the young med student/Yankees fan reemerge to fist me some more. Maybe his spirit fingers will help relieve the pressure.

They don't.

"Hmmm. . . . Nothing seems to be happening. Be back later."

No! Wait! Come back and fist me again! Maybe I'll dilate! Maybe something will happen. ANYTHING! OH GOD!

My OB shows up moments later to give me a nice pat on the forehead. "Your epi is on its way. I'm off to perform a C-section next door. I'll be back."

By the time the epi-dude comes in, I'm wailing. My contractions have no downtime. One on top of the other, and I cannot catch my breath. The doctors hold me down as epi-man shoots me up. Minutes later, convulsions aside, I am haaaaaaaapppppy. *Thhhhhhaaaaaaaank you kindly, man with neeeeeeeedle!*

I order several popsicles and wait for my next measurement. Hal lies down on the couch and is at once fast asleep with his feet on the sink. The room is quiet except for the faint sounds of Beck's "Sea Change" reverberating from my "birth mix tape." I count the tiny lines on the back of my hand and try to imagine what Archer is going to look like.

Suddenly my peaceful thoughts are destroyed by extreme pain.

"My epi's worn off!"

My screams wake Hal violently. He shoots up and runs out of the room to find a doctor and reappears with a really scary-looking nurse with no neck.

"It hasn't worn off," she says. "It hasn't even been an hour and a half!"

The nurse applies her latex glove and proceeds to fist me. She isn't nearly as gentle as the Yankees guy, but whatever. At this point, everyone is welcome in my vagina. *Hear ye! Hear ye! Vaginas are for lovers. Come one, come all!*

"Whoopsie-daisy! I can feel the head! You're having this baby *now!*"

"How is that possible? I was three centimeters dilated twenty minutes ago."

"Well, I'm not sure exactly. Unfortunately, you're going to have to wait a couple of minutes for your doctor to finish a cesarean next door."

Minutes later, my doctor arrives in his scrubs and mask. He pulls his stool up to my spread-eagle self and tells me to push before even saying hello.

"But wait! I'm not ready! What's happening?"

Apparently, there is no time to explain. My doctor strips down and out of his scrubs in seconds flat. He washes his hands and applies his gloves, all the while telling me that I'm a good girl. I keep reminding myself to think clinical, but even in childbirth I cannot detach myself from sex. Maybe I'm just immature. I'm afraid that I'm the only woman giving birth who cannot think of anything but how embarrassingly nonsexual it is to have five men staring into my abyss while I make animal sounds.

Our room suddenly erupts into chaos and I start pushing before I'm supposed to.

"Wait for me to give you the signal," he says. "Okay, and . . . go! Push!"

I push four times before my doctor asks if he can cut my vagisphere.

"I'm going to have to perform an episiotomy. Otherwise you will tear."

"Whatever, dude. Just . . . whatever."

Here goes nothing, I think. *This is the end of me and my adorably tidy and muscular vagina. I'll never be the same.*

I close my eyes. And then . . .

I open them. I watch in slow motion as the doctor holds up a tiny boy, still attached to me by a knotted strand of blue. I look over at Hal, who nearly faints onto the couch. There are tears in his eyes. The nurses are clapping and saying his name. *What's his name again? What's my name again? Where am I? Is that him? Is that my baby? Wait. Are you sure? Really? That just came out of . . . wait . . . really?*

The doctor places him in the tiny bassinet, and the room keeps right on spinning, revolving around the tiny boy who looks like an angel with squinty eyes. All I can hear are the sounds of the fluorescent lights buzzing and my heartbeat, like a drum. My breathing. In and out and *Oh my god*. In and out and *Oh my god*. The nurses are tending to Hal now, who is probably feeling as overwhelmed as me. I wish I could faint. I wish I could go to sleep. *What? Where am I again? What's the doctor saying to me? He has something in his hand. Oh, yeah. A baby. That's my baby boy. His name is Archer. That was the name we decided on and oh no . . . there is blood*. Blood is everywhere. All over the floor and on my hands, and *Gross get it off of me*. Does anyone have a towel?

"Here's your sun," the nurse says, and I wait for her to pull the sun out of the sky and hand it to me. But it isn't that kind of sun. Silly me. The sun is too big and hot to hold. She means the other kind of sun—my son. Yes, I'm a mother now—to a son. I close my eyes . . .

. . . and then I open them, and he is there. In my arms, and *Wait, does he know? Does he know that I'm his mother? Is he sure he wants to be my son? Am I sure? Did I really get pregnant? Maybe I'm dead and this is what happens when you die. Little boys are handed over to you and there is blood everywhere and* "Well, hello there. I'm your mommy. Can I shake your hand? Here, take my finger."

I feel strange. Like everyone is looking at me and I'm supposed to know how to work this thing. He looks like a gyro with a face because he is wrapped so tightly and is so small that I'm afraid I'll break him. *Wait! I don't have a license. Shouldn't I have a license?* Because you need a license to drive a car, and I think you even need one to go fishing, but I have a boy in my hands, and he's mine but I don't know how to work him. I don't know what gears to shift when. I don't know what to do with a fishing line.

Yesterday I was the daughter of my parents; today I am the mother of my sun or son or whatever he is. Probably a little of both.

"I'm going to sew you up now," the doctor says.

"Okay. Make sure you sew it tight."

The doctor laughs and shakes his head, but I'm serious. Because childbirth may be for vaginas, but Archer is out now. And he's beautiful and he's in my arms, and everything is perfect, except I'm consumed with my physical self and needing to know that weeks from now, after I heal and the blood stops and the stitches reattach what is now torn in half like paper, I will have my *pussy* back. My sex. My power. Nice and tight so that it's impossible to reach my heart or my womb without some effort.

"I want to feel brand-new, you know?"

Brand-new. Everything is brand-new. I close my eyes and hold on to my baby, numb from the waist down, guts all over the floor.

I stare into Archer's eyes and am at once hypnotized. My

head stops spinning, and the entire world moves in slow motion. I lie back in my hospital bed. Me, the patient. Me, the mother. Me, the bleeding womb of what it means to be woman. I touch my brand-new baby's wet hair.

TWO BECOMES
Three Becomes a Crowd

I HAD NO IDEA how messy this would be. I crouch on a latex glove full of ice, the hospital's makeshift diaper. I feel like my insides are going to pour out and spill down my leg. And it doesn't even matter—because of him. I climb onto my hospital bed, beside Archer who is supposed to be sleeping soundly in his bassinet. I pluck him out and put him on my chest and we breathe together in the recovery room. I'm exhausted but I can't sleep. I just want to stare at him. Understand him. Protect his eyes from the neon lights and his body from the cold.

Math has never been my strength, so I have a hard time figuring out how it is possible that two such imperfect people could create something so flawless.

$$\tfrac{1}{2} \text{ of me} + \tfrac{1}{2} \text{ of you} = 1 \text{ something perfect}$$

A hundred thousand times I wondered if he would look anything like me. Anything like his dad. Would he have our best features or our worst? My almond eyes and Hal's full pout? Or would he end up with my crooked nose and be prematurely bald. Would he inherit his father's sense of humor or his temper? Would he live up to his birth sign, a fellow Gemini like me, two-faced and torn, indecisive about whether to scream or whisper? Would he be an idealist, a dreamer? A make-believer? Or would he be more practical, like the men in his family? Would he grow to love poetry? Film? Miró? So many things I'd like to know. So many years ahead for us to find out.

I am especially in awe of Archer's cuticles, how they look like they could belong to a grown person even though he is only hours old, hours that separate him from his prelife. I wonder what he prefers: being inside of me or nestled under my arm. *This is what it feels like to love somebody,* I think. Because however I defined love before now seems so terribly off. So *not* like this.

When I look over at Hal, I know he knows. He takes my hand and I nod. And I think how from this moment forward, no matter what happens, Hal will be the only person in the world who understands the way I feel. The only person in the history of histories who can look at Archer with the same eyes, no matter how differently we may look at each other or the world.

We stare at each other, laughing and crying in disbelief, and I have never felt so close to anybody as I do right now with him, because we did this *together*. And I wonder if I will ever be able to match this feeling, this moment of physical discomfort and emotional high.

I want to just live here, in this hospital bed, in this moment. I don't want to leave. I don't want to go home. Because I know the house will soon be a mess and the nurse won't come in to check on me and wrap Archer up in his swaddling blankets. Because she's a professional and I'm just a new mom and I can't wrap him up as tight as she can and we're so comfortable right here and now, in our bubble world with vending machines and a red button that brings help. There will be no red buttons tomorrow. Or the next day.

We don't have to say anything aloud so we don't. We just stay up all night . . . except we don't have a baby to wait for anymore. Archer has arrived.

The only manual we've read up to this point has been for the car seat—the car seat that has been empty for the last month since we put it in the car. The car seat we can't for the life of us figure out how to use now that we have a baby to put in it. We argue and fuss, and I cry and Hal yells at me, and I get mad at him for being a dick.

"Here, let me try."

"No, let me!"

"But you're not doing it right!"

It takes us well over an hour to make sure Archer is in safely and the car seat is secure. We pull out of the parking garage and into the sun. I swallow tears and sit squashed against the door, watching out the window of my station wagon as the world speeds by. Two becomes three becomes crazy becomes our new life.

Archer's a week old. His hands are neatly folded under his slightly jaundiced chin, and his breath sounds like a tide. In and out and once in a while a sneeze. I say "Bless you" from the other room and check in on him every few minutes. Sometimes when he sneezes milk comes out his nose. The same thing happens to me when I sneeze, but I always thought it was because I had my adenoids removed when I was six. Archer is just a newborn. Maybe he doesn't have adenoids yet.

Sometimes when he is sleeping I watch him dream. He moves his eyebrows and reaches his hands up toward the sky, and every day there is a new skill or instinct or expression, and it's sort of like falling in love except a thousand times more intense and a million times more frightening. And even at 5:00 AM when he is wailing to be held, fed, changed, spitting milk on my clothes, I am so overwhelmed with love that it doesn't matter.

My mother was right when she said, "Just you wait! You'll

know how it feels to be a mother. To be me!" It was the epilogue of every argument over curfew, her explanation for hysteria after I pierced my face, after I cursed at the dinner table, after I got caught smoking pot. "You will have a baby one day, and you will understand." When Archer was born and my mother entered the birthing room and saw me with my baby for the first time, she raised her eyebrows and said, "See. Do you understand now?"

It's difficult to fathom that one day Archer will be a man, a teen-ager, a little boy who plays with Tonka trucks and crawls through the grass in the park. He is so tiny and vulnerable and helpless. But every day he sheds more skin, and one day he will outgrow his shell like a hermit crab, too big for a bassinet, a crib, a twin bed, our house. Today Archer is a week old, and in many ways I am too. Everything looks different now, a lighter shade. I am just a baby myself, I think, and now I have one. *A baby! In my arms!* I pinch myself and wipe my eyes, and he's still there, between my legs with his head on my knees, waving his hands. A new life has changed mine. I now know what it means to really give birth, not just to an idea but to a perfect little being with big gray eyes and miniature hands. I'm crazy in love and scared out of my mind because the world is so fucked-up and jaded and my baby is so new and perfect and I want to protect him from the monsters. Just like my mother wanted to do for me, and her mother for her, and every mother through time.

The ecstasy can only be matched by the agony: The hell that has come with our tiny angel. The rift in our family. The tearing of our hearts from one another, exhausted and frustrated and totally clueless.

Archer won't sleep. He just screams and cries and won't eat, and I just want to go to bed but I can't. Even when it's quiet and I get into bed and close my eyes, I'm wide awake and then the second I doze off, Archer's awake and it's my job to stop his cries. I have to know what to do. I pace the living room with the bedroom door closed and the windows shut and the fan blowing on our faces.

"I can't handle this," Hal says.

"It's only been three weeks!"

"We should give him up for adoption. Seriously, I can't live this way."

"You're such an asshole. Take it back!"

"No! This is royally fucked."

"*You* are the one who's fucked!"

Suddenly I feel like I have two screaming babies, except one of them I want to protect and the other I want to kill.

"I hate you so much right now!"

I sound like I'm twelve but I don't care. I'm pissed off. I'm crazy. I feel like I'm all alone even though I haven't had a moment to myself in weeks, since before Archer was born. I'm screaming as loud as I can, and in my head all I keep thinking is *What the fuck have I done! WHAT THE FUCK AM I DOING HERE! With two strange boys in my house! And where am I? Is this supposed to feel like home?* Half of my boxes aren't even unpacked.

I feel the need to escape. "I'm going to take a walk," I say, but before I do, I write a list of things for Hal to do if the baby wakes up. I make sure he knows where everything is and how it works before I go. Then I slowly close the front door behind me so I don't wake Archer.

I emerge from my cocoon and enter a world that stinks of exhaust and cigarettes and homeless people. Then I think, *I want one.* A cigarette. Not a homeless person.

I walk full speed toward the 7-Eleven on 3rd Street and Gardner. I cross the street with my giant diaper bag over my shoulder. Because this is what my purse looks like now. A giant diaper bag with crap sticking out and pacifiers hanging off the straps from clamped lanyards. Diapers and wipes and blankets and beanies and bottles and maxi pad diapers for me to bleed all over.

The same couple are working the register—the ones I bought the beef jerky from that made me sick.

I'm afraid one of my neighbors will see me and think I'm trashy for buying cigarettes the week after my baby was born. *Mothers who smoke are disgusting,* I think, but I hardly care at this point. I need a cigarette. I just can't let anyone see me smoking. I pull my hoodie over my head and buy a pack of Parliament Lights and escape out the back door before anyone can see me or give me back my change.

The alley is empty and smells of garbage and oil puddles. I take a seat. I unwrap the plastic from my box and search my diaper bag for a lighter.

"Goddamitmotherfuckerwhatthefuckahhhhh!!"

I burst into tears. It's too much, and *What am I doing and who do I think I am and why am I here? Behind 7-Eleven with my cigarettes and no lighter? What life am I living and where do I belong?* This is my life, I think. My life without a lighter in my pocket and sleepless nights. Will I someday understand or at least get used to this? Will I ever sleep? Where have all my friends gone? I want my mom. I miss being taken care of. I want to go to my old bedroom in my parents' house on Corte Cardo Street with the dried-out roses in the window and the painting of the giant bird above my bed. And I want to sleep and dream and wake up sixteen again with my old high school boyfriend and my boxer shorts and flat belly and my diary with the list of things I want to do before I turn twenty-five and the ability to believe that it's still possible to do them.

I flag down a rocker chick with pink dreads and striped tights under an orange tutu. She's smoking, so I ask her if I could borrow a light. She hands me her cigarette and I press her ember to my Parliament until it's lit. Our eyes meet as I'm inhaling, and she looks away. Face to face with my past, I ask her for her name.

"Rachel," she says.

Rachel is also my sister's name, a name I have been going by since she was born and relatives starting confusing us.

"I'm Rebecca."

"Oh," she says before taking her cigarette back and walking away.

I crouch behind the trash bin and inhale long drags, holding my breath and exhaling rings. I was never able to form a ring unless no one was looking. I was never able to do anything well unless no one was looking. Like sing or explain my point of view. I finish the cigarette, but not before I light a second with my own cherry and head home.

I take the long way across La Brea, past the furniture stores. I try not to look at myself in the reflection of glass windows, but it's almost impossible to look ahead when you're not alone. And I can't shake the ghost of Christmas past, pink-haired in striped tights, a girl with a name that has always been confused with mine.

I quietly unlock the front door and wearily make my way inside. Hal's asleep on the couch with his feet up, and Archer's asleep in his swing beside him. I sit down next to my husband and take his hand. He smiles, half-sleeping, and opens one eye.

"You okay?" he asks.

"Yeah. Are you?"

"I think so."

"Me too. I love you."

"I love you too," he says.

He doesn't say anything about how I smell like cigarettes. He just closes his eyes and scoots over so that I can lie beside him. So that we can be close again. He smells my hair and wraps his arm around my waist and I get lost in the sounds of stillness, the sweeping whoosh of the swing, back and forth and back again, the tick of the wall clock that counts the seconds of peace and quiet like a child counts cracks in the sidewalk.

I know this isn't going to be easy. There will be times when I will hate myself and my husband and maybe even Archer. Times when I'll want to be alone and won't be able to. Times like right this second, when I just want to get in my car and head north, merge onto the 101 and drive up the coast, to a rustic shack in Big Sur where I can hide out and write and swear and smoke. But that's the other side of what it means to be in love. To be passionate is to momentarily fantasize about throwing it all away.

Hal and I lock tired eyes in bed as Archer sleeps peacefully on the pillow between us. We both know this is going to be difficult and scary, and a certain sadness permeates as we come to accept that our wild fling has ended suddenly. We're parents now. We have crossed the threshold of grownupsville, population: 3. We have entered a new phase in our lives with new rules and assumptions and lines we mustn't cross and things we shouldn't say and sleep-deprived nights.

We know the little boy nestled between us now relies on us to show him the ropes and set a good example and love him unconditionally, that we will make plenty of mistakes trying to find our way as parents and as a family but we can do it. *We have to be able to do it.*

"Half of me plus half of you equals this perfect person," I say to myself, and I know that Hal is thinking the same thing.

We reach our hands across our sleeping baby to hold each other, but Archer startles, so Hal takes his hand back and puts it under his pillow, and I take my hand back and put it under mine. The baby is finally asleep and the last thing we want to do is wake him. So we lie together, separated by the life that sleeps peacefully between us and all that has come with his arrival.

TO LIVE
and Diet in L.A.

I'VE BEEN BACK TO WORK since Archer was one week old. We're completely broke and need the money. Our insurance has gone up again, and neither Hal nor I have the kind of job where we are entitled to benefits, so I'm back to interviewing nude coeds while I pump breastmilk from the two ducts that work. I'm back to copywriting and working as a chat host for a nonprofit organization while running around the house with Archer in the Bjorn and folders of magazine queries on my desktop.

I'm lucky that I get to work from home, but I'm also lonely here. Maybe this is it for me. I'll be like the mom in *What's Eating Gilbert Grape,* working from the comfort of my couch, morbidly obese and unable to move without assistance. Making babies, inhaling recycled air in a room with closed windows

The local market has a scale in the pharmacy. I wait until I'm alone, insert my quarter, and wait for the truth. The scale reads 182 pounds at six weeks postpartum. I'm fat—and not with a "p-h."

"What did the scale say?" Hal asks.

I tell him "One seventy-one."

"Not bad! You're doing great!"

I feel bad about lying, but I can't bear the truth. I've only lost two pounds since the initial eighteen that came off with the water and the blood and the baby. It wouldn't be so bad if I weren't waking up every morning at 6:00 AM after fifteen minutes total sleep to go hiking in Celebrityville. Nothing makes a fat woman feel like more of a fat woman than walking backward uphill next to Jessica Alba. *Oh and there goes Kate Bosworth with Orlando Bloom.* Skinny women are one thing. Famous and grotesquely beautiful skinny women are enough to make a postpartum woman suicidal.

I bring Archer with me, not because Hal can't take care of him while I'm gone, but because I want to have an obvious excuse for looking this way. And a Baby Bjorn full of infant does the trick. At least that is what I tell myself.

Hal has weight to lose too. Apparently men get fat along with their pregnant counterparts. Together we gained one hundred pounds and have the remains of one broken chair to prove it.

Three days after we came home from the hospital, I made a conscious decision to break my doctor's orders and exercise immediately. Instead of driving, I walked everywhere, sometimes miles, to the beauty supply store and the coffee shop and Whole Foods with Archer in his stroller and defrosted Morningstar Farms sausage hanging from plastic grocery bags in soggy boxes.

When Archer was five days old, we walked to Samy's Camera on Fairfax to drop off some film. I had spent the better part of the first few days posing him on my knees and taking photos of his shining eyes for use in baby announcements.

"Wow! Your baby is so teensy-tiny!" a woman shrieked, peering into the stroller.

"He's a newbie," I said. "He'll be one week old on Saturday."

It was Thursday, so the woman quickly did the math on her fingers.

"He's five days old? And you're already taking him out?"

"Well, we're just on a walk. We live in the neighborhood."

I kind of lied. We were at least a mile away from home, which in Los Angeles is like walking from the moon to Jupiter.

"You shouldn't be out with your baby this early. It's dangerous."

"Not as dangerous as living cooped up indoors with no air-conditioning in the middle of summer," I wanted to say, but I didn't. I also wanted to point out that in other parts of the world, mothers go back to work with their babies strapped to their chests days after giving birth, and rather than taking advice from strangers, a woman is better off trusting her instincts. Mine were to get the fuck out of the house and burn some calories.

I guess new mothers and their new babies aren't supposed to go for early morning hikes either, because once again, I am accosted by a neighborhood dog-walker as I transfer Archer from his car seat to my Baby Bjorn.

"Your baby is so young to be out in this dust."

Apparently these are the rules based on studies I don't care to read, because sitting on my ass with a book or on the Internet is not an option for me right now. I'm fat. And I'd rather hemorrhage while stretching at the top of Runyan Canyon, because I live in Hollywood, where size 6 is considered plus-size, and not even my right thigh could fit into a size 6.

Everyone on the hill is rooting me on as I huff and puff, climbing the steepest part of the trail backward to work my ass and upper thighs.

"You can do it!"

"Go mama, go!"

It feels good to have highly attractive cheerleaders, but it also feels awful knowing I'm the underdog. People root for the underdog because they feel sorry for her, and the last thing I want is for people to feel sorry for me. I want people to hate me because I'm beautiful. I want people to be jealous, threatened. I am a woman, after all.

"You've become obsessed," Hal says. "You need to get some sleep. You've become fanatical."

I'm not fanatical. I'm just shallow and insecure and unable to face my reflection. And there is a difference.

I was never skinny enough growing up in Southern California, surrounded by beautiful women. There were size 0s, 2s, and 4s, and then there was me. Rocking a size 8, I always felt like the fat one. I never shared clothes with any of my friends. My legs were too long. My waist too short. My boobs too big. My arms flabby. I never had a perfect body, and I hated myself every day of my young adult life because of it, measuring myself against my own irrational standard of beauty. That changed when I became pregnant. I fell in love with my body as it swelled with life. I loved knowing that everything I put in my body I was giving my unborn child. I felt like a woman, and for the first time I accepted my weight instead of obsessing over it. I completely and totally let go, and it was an incredible relief.

Now I feel differently. I feel empty and saggy and bloated and *all alone in here*, under skin and bones and flab. I'm in search of a new shell. My ego has grown too big for the one I currently inhabit. I have disappeared into the background of my perfect son's shadow. Everywhere we go they look at him.

They can't help it, I think. *He's perfect.*

And he is. He smiles at strangers and clutches his little teddy bear and his toes curl and he makes little sounds and giggles when you say, "Ahhhh-boo!" And when people turn their heads after us, it's for him. Always for him.

I catch myself gazing at the buxom blonde of my youth in old photos, thirteen years old, posed on my best friend's dad's Harley-Davidson in my bikini and borrowed high heels, as my friend snapped away on her disposable camera. We were clueless then, unaware of the crowd of dirty old men we were drawing out onto their balconies from across the street, visible in the background of the photographs. I never noticed them until now.

"Oh to be young again," I say, as if I have lived a thousand years. As if the photos I can't stop staring at are sepia-stained and curling at the edges.

I remember how one day I went from being a girl to a woman, and how weird it sounded: Woman. *Woman.* It was always hard for me to act as a bystander to my own changing of the guard. Going from girlfriend to wife for example. From "chick" to "mom." From "This is my friend Rebecca" to "This is Archer's mom."

Apparently, being a mother makes me different. I'm sleeping with a baby on my chest, and suddenly I am someone new.

Of course, I've been far too busy gazing into Archer's gray eyes and biting his toes to recognize who I've become. I do know for certain that I am overwhelmed and sleep deprived and obsessing over the one thing I know I can control in this new and out-of-control life: My body. My weight. I must do what I can to make myself look like I used to before all of this. When I wasn't a mom or a wife or a girlfriend. When I was free and fresh and had a lifetime of possibilities and open doors. When I had complete control, or at the very least believed with my heart that I did.

I come home from an afternoon of walking, first to the L.A. County Museum of Art and the La Brea Tar Pits and then up to Pan Pacific Park. My feet are sore, and I've been chugging water since this morning. Bottle after bottle, trying to wash the fat away.

Archer is asleep in his stroller, so I tiptoe to the bedroom closet and begin to unpack the boxes of my pre-pregnancy wardrobe. I steer straight for my favorite jeans, folded badly, with a crease down the right pant leg. I shake them out and press them flat with my hands. They smell like a boy's bedroom, musky and a bit like cardboard.

I strip down to my underwear and lie down on the bed. I wriggle into them and try with all my might to pull them up around my hips, but I can't. I suck in. I hold my breath.

"Come on, come on, come on. . . . " I say.

But my jeans aren't listening.

Later that night Hal asks me what happened. The skin on my hip is scratched, and my waist is belted by a black-and-blue bruise.

"My jeans still don't fit," I say and he hugs me.

"You're still beautiful to me."

I smile and thank him.

If only that were enough.

According to the women on the message boards, breastfeeding is supposed to help you lose the weight, but everyone I've talked to has claimed otherwise:

"I didn't lose a single pound until I weaned my baby."

So I guess there is hope for me yet, now that I have been advised to quit breastfeeding because my milk production sucks. I pumped for four hours last night and only managed four ounces. One ounce per hour is not a whole lot, especially when the milk is pink from being strained out of bloody nipples.

I want to cry as I pour the precious serum down the drain, but I have no choice.

A mother should not feed her child bloody breastmilk, I don't care what the La Leche League says. Bloody breast is *not* best.

I pack up my Medela pump and all of my various paraphernalia and try not to feel bad about not being able to breastfeed. I was told I couldn't do it from the start, and I defied the odds by breastfeeding even a tiny bit. I should be proud of myself. But when people on the street ask me why I'm not breastfeeding or eye me when I tear open a tube of Enfamil and mix it with a bottle of water, I freeze. I don't want anyone to think I am a bad mother, so I find myself explaining myself to strangers in line at the bookstore or local Starbucks. I tell my story to mommies at the park when they whip out their breasts to feed their babies as I rummage through my diaper bag for my bag of formula. It's hard not to feel guilty when you're a mother.

I'm sobbing like a lunatic, pacing the house with Archer in my arms, except this time I'm crying with joy. I'm elated. Proud and overwhelmed and laughing between tears because a glorious thing has just happened: My jeans finally fit. My breasts are back to their normal size and *Oh my god. My jeans actually fit me!*

I was so afraid to weigh myself that I waited until Archer's six-month pediatrician appointment to get on the scale. I'm five pounds away, but it doesn't even matter because I'm in my old jeans. And they look amazing. They look so amazing in fact that Archer and I are going to head over to Amoeba to strut our stuff for the hot dirty-haired record store boys.

I apply a full face of makeup and shimmy into my favorite Marc Jacobs top—*Oh, holy shit! It fits!*—and then I take the straightening iron to my hair and spritz a spray or two of perfume at my chest, and we're off.

On the way to Amoeba, with the windows down and my wind-blown hair stuck to my lip gloss, I feel good. I feel like myself again. And then?

A man in a beat-up Bronco pulls up beside me, rolls down his window, and says, "Cute baby. You want another, cuz I'd be happy to give you one if you'd like."

Sure it's rude and perverted, and the dude is old and has a back seat full of empty soda cans, but I am still tempted to put my car in park and go make out with him in the middle of the street.

I guess one woman's sexual harasser is another woman's hero.

GROWNUPS

"JUST A CITY BOY, born and raised on South Detroit Street,"
Hal bellows, pounding his Clavanova with sarcastic fervor. We
have been enduring Hal's piano ballads since Archer was in utero.

"No more Journey," I tell him. The two of us are packing our
stuff, side by side, cutting tape and placing our books and stacks of
CDs in stained Trader Joe's boxes.

"Don't say it," he pleads. "The Journey comes with us. I'll
leave behind the Poison. But the Journey comes with."

My husband has a thing for hair metal. Maybe because he has
no hair.

I almost feel like an adult right now, playing house as I label
the taped boxes for the move to our new two-bedroom duplex,
almost three times the size of this place. We found a house that we
love on a tree-lined street in Larchmont Village, in the southern

part of Hollywood. Our new house will have a yard. And room to park the cars. And a bedroom to ourselves. The rent is nearly twice what we've been paying, but we can't stay here any longer. If we do, we will likely kill each other or die from inhaling mold spores that our landlord refuses to eradicate. Plus, Hal has been promoted.

Hal works in television, where work is typically seasonal, so today's promotion might be tomorrow's unemployment—but the bigger risk is staying here. There just isn't enough room for all of us.

I don't know why this move feels so different—I feel like I'm maturing with every box I label with my Sharpie. I shake the pen and feel my skin thin. My hair gray. This is the seventh time I've moved in the six years I've lived in Los Angeles, but this time we aren't just moving. We're moving on, no matter how lopsided and unpredictable the future might seem. We're changing the scene. For the good of our family. Leaving single life behind— growing up.

I can't help feeling a little sad, even if I hate this apartment and its mold spores and the neighbors upstairs who apparently are into jumping rope in platform shoes at 3:00 AM, dropping hammers and paperweights all night just for fun, making sleep an impossible task—even when the baby isn't screaming..

And just as I pack the parcels of our soon-to-be-former domicile with pots and pans and clothes and books and Hal's guitars, I realize that I am leaving part of me behind. My skin is in the dust that gathers in the corners and on the ceiling fan. My fingerprints linger in the invisible words I scribbled madly on the pink tile of the shower. I will take a part of this apartment with me as well: the splinters from the broken door, the foot fungus from the mildewed shower, the yellow paint stains on my favorite sweatpants from our household paintathon. I secretly love this apartment as much as I despise it. Hal and I spent our honeymoon here, after all, spooning on the couch, my belly round with Archer, *the womb of the unknown soldier*. There was the night we paced the apartment, impatiently waiting for me to be induced, Hal with his camcorder in my face, zooming in and out at my swollen body while I covered my face with my hands. We have spent the first six months of Archer's life here—some of the most emotionally charged months of my life—and the butterflies flap around in my chest as I pull dust bunnies from Archer's hair.

I revel in the memories, tracing the corners of the rooms with my eyes: Coffeemaker and vegetable steamer unplugged and taped together haphazardly. The pot we boil the bottles in, stained with calcium deposits from the tap water. The calendar with the x's slashing its expired days.

The baby swing glides, and Archer's little head falls to the side. I lift it, and it falls again. So I leave him be.

At six months old, Archer will finally have his own room. The crib, kept in its box in our closet, will soon be assembled: the last of the shower gifts opened and in use.

My family comes up to help us move, just as they always have. My mom is waiting at our new apartment with a carload of boxes I've had stored in my parents' garage, and my grandmother has come to help me organize my kitchen. They are here because they love us and want to help us and are willing to drop everything to do so.

One day when you have children of your own, you will understand.

"Here, hand me that," my mother says.

I hand over the giant canvas I painted of Hal and me with the keys around our necks, and she carries it up the steps. I unlock Archer's infant seat and lift him over the threshold of our new apartment. My grandmother is on her knees in the kitchen unwrapping vases and glasses and throwing the newspaper away. She places bowls on the counters and leans over to kiss Archer's bare toes when I place him down beside her.

Three generations of mothers.

"My little Bubula!" Grandma says.

"Sweet baby," my mother coos, combing Archer's hair with her fingers.

"Little sleepybear."

My ex-roommate Frank appears from out of nowhere with his box cutter and a bouquet of stargazers.

"Happy housewarming!" he declares, and I kiss his cheeks. "I love it here! It's fabulous!" He drags me to the back of the house. Frank lives for volunteering his services, offering his knack for furniture assembly like an enthusiastic helper elf.

"What do you think?" Frank asks. "Should we put the crib against the window, or would the dresser look more fantabulous there?" Frank drags the crib box through the door and carries it back to Archer's room.

"Archer should have a view of the garden," he demands, his hands on his hips in typical Frank fashion.

Frank loves gardens. Our patio in our old apartment was overflowing with his flourishing foliage.

I push the crib up against the wall.

"Perfection," he smiles.

And suddenly our new house feels like a home. With dear Frank arranging the drapes on the windows and my mother nailing paintings in the walls and my grandmother playing peekaboo with Archer and Hal and my father bringing in all of the heavy furniture. And here we are.

"Trick or treat!"

I have forgotten about Halloween. I'm not prepared.

"There is no candy in the house," I tell the kids. "I'm sorry."

"Don't go to that house," I hear them warn from the sidewalk. "No candy there."

I have failed as an adult in a neighborhood where children trick-or-treat. But I've never had children at my door before. How was I to know?

When Hal comes home, I'm seated in the middle of the room, in the dark, with Archer asleep beside me on the floor.

"Did all the light bulbs burn out?"

I shake my head. "It's Halloween. No candy. We forgot the Halloween candy! We're terrible adults."

"No we're not. We're just moving!"

"We need to learn how to multitask!" I wail.

"How could we have known that this was L.A.'s premier trick-or-treating neighborhood?"

Outside, children are playing on our new street, chasing each other on bikes in their goblin costumes. The air smells of Korean barbeque, and the trees blow wild, combing the squeals of children's laughter with their leaves.

This is what it feels like to grow up, I think. To be an adult. Except, I don't feel grown up. Not really. I feel like a child, actually. Like a little awkward girl on the outskirts of adulthood—watching the grownups chat among themselves. It isn't because they're older. Or because I feel I might not have anything in common with them. It's because I don't know where I'm supposed to stand. I'm in limbo—

overwhelmed by the swarm of parents that suddenly surround me. Afraid I will get sucked in and swallowed by the stereotypes I'm not ready to accept.

Leave me alone. I'm not ready for playdates and neighborhood watch. I can't even remember Halloween candy!

And suddenly I'm panicked. What if I can't find people like me? Mothers who are new at "all of this," who can help me define what "all of this" even means?

I want to be accepted, and yet it wasn't long ago that I looked at young mothers and thought, *What a waste!* I realize now how my friends must look at me.

"You have a kid? No fucking way. When did you . . . "

"He's almost seven months."

"Wow. Crazy."

"Yeah. So how have you been?"

"Fine. Yeah. Um . . . okay . . . so . . . take care. I'll call you. Or whatever. Okaythenbye."

I guess everyone is afraid of growing up. And maybe that makes my old friends afraid of me. And maybe that makes me, at times, a little afraid of myself. It isn't that I want to be a child again or even a party girl. I just want to feel comfortable at the adult table. Or better yet, I just want a table to sit at. Somewhere I can bring Archer and not feel totally alone.

Hal and I wait in the darkness, together, until the voices disappear and the knocks and doorbell rings stop. We look around our new house—at the table we picked out and the chairs that don't match but do and the hutch my mother found at a swap meet, full of my old books. And the baby swing filled with our new baby.

"What do you think?" Hal finally asks, nudging me.

"I think I like it here," I say.

And I mean it.

"It's starting to feel like home," he agrees.

"It *is* home."

UNDER
Pressure

On our way home from the grocery store at dusk, an old woman stops us at the intersection of 3rd and La Brea. She's muttering at me, so I assume the mangy, mustache-cursed woman needs my help. Maybe she's lost and needs directions. Maybe she's about to have a heart attack and needs me to call an ambulance.

"Is there something I can help you with?" I ask.

"Heylowwww missus. Your child no see at this time. Light bad for eyes!"

"Excuse me?"

"Yaaaaaaah! Zis light makes bad eye for child. You cover the face like zeeeees!"

The little old lady pulls Archer's stroller shade over his body, making sure he is completely sheltered from the harsh rays of sunset and streetlamps.

"What the hell are you doing? He's fine."

"Wha? No! Cover eyes. It's bad from streetlights go bright. He go blind!"

"I think he will live. Thanks."

She shrugs and pouts. "Fine. You are ze bad mother. Bad, bad mother."

The light turns green and I flee to the other side of the boulevard, even though the red hand isn't blinking and the walk man isn't there. The old wife chases after us, her outstretched pointer finger wrinkled in the lamplight.

I rush home as the sound of her voice fades in the distance: "Bad, bad mother. He go blind! Bad mother . . . "

If I have learned anything in these last eight months, it's that when old ladies flag me down from across a busy intersection, I should keep walking. They do not need help crossing the street.

Maybe it used to take a village to raise a child, but that was long before the village was made up of so many idiots. Everywhere I turn, I am inundated with judgment. Strangers and friends and family members, books in hand, full of advice and recipes and tales of yore. From the little old women on La Brea Avenue to old men in line at Barnes & Noble.

I have a new respect for mothers who not only handle the pressures of motherhood but dodge tips from a myriad of magazines and books and women who climb up on pedestals with unsolicited advice. I look into my fellow mothers' bloodshot eyes and nod. *I understand.*

I cross my fingers behind my back and say, "I'm fine, just fine," when anyone asks me how I'm doing. I smile, even though I feel like I'm folding like paper, slowly ripping at the edges from the wet heat of the pressure cooker. *What if I can't do it all?*

Humpty Dumpty sat on a wall. Humpty Dumpty had a great fall. . . .

I take Archer out of his crib and into my arms.

"You're supposed to be sleeping, baby."

It's amazing how fast he stops crying when I pick him up. It is still hard to believe his cries are for me. Because he needs *me*. A feeling both wonderful and completely terrifying.

"How about you lie back down and go to sleep so mama can unpack the kitchen, okay?"

I want to be taken care of, and at the same time I want so badly to be able to take care of myself. And I can't. I want to help everyone, but I can't. I want to show Archer that life is not perfect, that the world is wild and unorthodox and there is beauty in the dark and *Here, let's eat sand all day and finger paint with icecream. . . .* Yet all the while, I hold in my hands a box of wet wipes. Antibacterial. You can never be too careful.

Yes you can!

No you cannot.

These days I care about the kinds of things I never dreamed I'd even think about. I care about jobs providing benefits. I care about money and lifestyle and keeping a clean house, an orderly life. And it's consuming me. There are days when I get in my car to go to the gym, and for a split second I think about turning right instead of left, of taking the 101 to San Francisco to join the street performers (I could play the tambourine!). So much of my energy is spent trying to catch up with my life and outrun it at the same time. *Faster, so it all blurs. Faster, and I can be spontaneous again. I can be free. Selfish. I can wander aimlessly. I can feel lost.*

Sometimes I miss the yesterdays. The guts. *But the guts are still here! They have to be.*

Maybe. I can turn myself inside out, but a part of me is afraid that when I do, I will find a clean interior, wires tied neatly in a bow, and I cannot imagine a scarier sight. White-picket-fenced. Responsible. Shoot me, then, in the foot. Watch me bleed. *No thanks. I don't want a Band-Aid.*

Growing up, my mom was very much together. She never cussed. She never flipped anyone off. She never broke the law. Or snuck out for a cigarette. But I am not my mother. I am myself. And while I want what's best for my child, I also want what's best for me.

Make everything seem easy: life and parenthood and marriage and free-lancing for pennies, writing a novel and smiling after a rejection, keeping the faith after two, reminding yourself that four years of work counted for a lot, counted for everything. Make the bed. Make it nice. Make the people laugh when you sit down to write, and if you can't make them laugh, make them cry.

Make them want to hug you or hold you or punch you in the face. Make them want to kill you or fuck you or be your friend. Make them change. Make them happy. Make the baby smile. Make him laugh. Make him dinner. Make him proud. Hold the phone, someone is on the other line. She says it's important. People are dying. Children. Friends. Press MUTE, *because there is nothing you can say. Press* OFF, *because you're running out of minutes. Running out of time. Soon the baby will be grown up, and you'll regret the time you spent pushing him away for one more paragraph in the manuscript no one will ever read. Remember who you are now. Wait. Remember who you were. Wait. Remember what's important. Make a list. Ten things—no, twenty. Twenty thousand things you want to do before you die, but what if tomorrow never comes? No one will remember. No one will know. No one will laugh or cry or make the bed. No one will have a clue which songs to sing to the baby. No one will be there for the children. No one will finish the first draft of the novel. No one will publish the one that's been finished for months. No one will remember the thought you had last night, that great idea you forgot to write down.*

It's time I came to terms with the truth instead of beating myself up with italicized thoughts. Who am I to feel overwhelmed when Atlas is out there, floating in space with the weight of the world on his shoulders? His legs crooked and veiny like branches, his feet sinking deeper into nothing. There are pencils in my ears and ideas in my head and pacifiers in my shoes. There is throw-up in my hair where there used to be perfume. How can I be everything? *It isn't possible,* I tell myself. *Just let go.*

I try not to cry in front of Archer, and when Hal and I fight, we try our best to whisper-yell so as not to wake him or scare him or teach him. I want to protect him from our words and the tears that occur as a result. But today I can't help it—I'm on the stoop of our apartment, breaking down.

And all I keep thinking is that sometimes it sucks being a mom and a wife. Sometimes the pressure is too much. Sometimes I just want to be alone. Have my old life back. Sometimes I think, *How did I get here, and who are these strangers in my house?*

Archer looks up at me. I'm trying to hide my face from him but it's too late. He frowns, his bottom lip quivering.

"No, please don't cry," I say. "Mommy's okay, dude. Everything's fine."

But he knows. Because his chest is pressed against my heart and he just knows. He leans back, takes the pacifier from his mouth and the blankie from his shoulder, and gives them to me. Because when he cries, that's what I do. I give him his blankie and his pacifier, and within minutes he's smiling again.

And so I sit—with mascara down to my ankles, a pacifier in my mouth, and a red blankie over my head.

Yes! This is exactly what I need, I think.

"Thank you, Archer."

I pull the blankie off my face and there, in front of me, is my perfect baby boy, smiling with his eyes.

And at once I forget about everything that has thrown me from my horse, and moments later I too am smiling again.

"Cute baby," says a woman with a stroller who's stopped at the bottom of the steps. Her daughter looks about Archer's age, and she is squinting from the sun. *If only the old woman of La Brea were here,* I think.

"I'm Rebecca," I say. "And this is Archer."

"I'm Kate, and this is Franny. We live down the street."

We exchange small talk about the neighborhood and not getting enough sleep. She's a work-at-home mom too.

"It's overwhelming, isn't it," she says.

I nod. "But worth it, right?"

She nods back.

The secret handshake.

Franny starts to cry, and Kate shakes her head.

"It was nice to meet you," she says.

I wave with Archer's tiny hand. "Maybe we'll see you around."

Maybe Humpty Dumpty was never the same. Maybe he climbed back on the wall without an arm or a foot or an ear and looked upon a new view, from a different side of the wall, and maybe he was happy there. Maybe he realized that just because he was a work in progress didn't mean he had to hide his weaknesses, fill the missing pieces haphazardly. Perhaps he was whole in a new way.

MONSTERS
under the Bed

I STAND IN MY OLD second-grade classroom with my second-grade teacher, kind-eyed and gray-haired. Every year since I graduated from high school, I've come home to San Diego to teach his students a poetry lesson. I read them old poems and ask questions and write words on the dry erase board where a chalkboard used to be.

"A word is worth a thousand pictures," I tell them.

They start drawing.

The classroom seems smaller every year I come to speak to Mr. R's class. Some of the children from last year return to say hello and ask me to sign an autograph on their arm. They think I am famous because I live in Los Angeles and once wrote some stories for a teen book series, because I was the homecoming queen at the high school up the street.

"Will you sign my T-shirt?" one of them asks.

"I'm afraid you might get into trouble."

"I don't care."

I listen to the children as they tell me about their favorite stories and how when they grow up they want to be writers too. We write a poem together about the beach, and soon after, the bell rings and the children scurry out for recess, leaving me alone with my old teacher.

I ask him how everything is, and he shrugs. "There are new rules," he says. He explains that two children were suspended a month ago for kissing on the playground. Mr. R senses my shock and shakes his head.

"It's really sad what's happening," he darkens. "People are so afraid these days."

I tell him about my kindergarten class, and how there was a little boy and his name was Michael and we used to kiss under the slide. It was the beginning of boys and flirting and tingles, and I wouldn't have traded my awkward bliss for anything. Not even ice cream on a summer day.

"The boy was suspended for a week," he repeats.

"For kissing?"

Mr. R. nods his head. "Sexual harassment. Only seven years old."

I don't know what to say. I imagine Archer as a little boy, a seven-year-old version of myself, chasing girls around and kissing their arms. I imagine getting a call from the school principal: "Your child is sexually harassing little girls on the playground."

"I don't believe it," I say.

"They're just kids," he whispers, his hands in his hair.

We both stare at the wall and say nothing. I am shocked. Who writes such a rule book, punishing children for being curious? Punishing little boys for being little boys. I try not to think about it, but my heart is on fire. *Seven-year-old boy. Sexual harassment. What is happening?*

Has the innocence of youth been so poisoned by fear? There used to be monsters under the bed, and now they are among us, terrified of the world and unable to function without pressing charges and pointing fingers and keeping children separate from one another.

I feel like I am going to be sick.

I leave the classroom at the bell and walk out to my car. And I drive past what used to be cow fields, where my friends and I used to pick dandelions and look for four-leaf clovers, the hidden valley where I smoked my first cigarette, the wetland where I used to follow the neighborhood boys in the summer. My friend Kelsey and I called it fairyland. Not anymore. No more fairylands and meadows or cow fields. These places have long since gone. Now it's a hillside covered with tract homes. A meadow covered with tract homes. A wetland, dry and dead, covered with tract homes.

I drive toward the beach, park, and climb to the viewpoint, taking a seat on a memorial bench, in loving memory of a boy from my class who died. *The past has passed.* We used to make out on the bluff at dusk, bare feet dangling over the sand. The bluff is now blocked off.

Private Property. Keep Out.

Danger, Keep Away.

I watch a group of tall blondes in bikinis. I remember when I used to look like that. Tall, tan, and busty with long yellow hair tangled in my bathing suit ties. I watch them without being seen. I could watch for hours and they wouldn't notice me. I am quiet these days. Pale, smaller in bust, larger in thigh, hair darker and longer, practically unrecognizable.

I try to relate to the scene playing out beneath me. The girls. The place. The time. But I cannot. They are supposed to be my past, but in them I see nothing. Not a trace of my youth. I find it odd, disheartening even. I lean against the sign. Danger. You might fall off the edge.

Is this my home? Children suspended for kissing. Fields bulldozed for tract homes. Flower fields replaced with strip malls. Starbucks and PetSmart and Bed Bath & Beyond. There used to be ponds teeming with crawdads and playgrounds to kiss boys on.

A picture is worth a thousand words. A thousand thoughts. A thousand questions. I was a child here, in the dirt and the sea and the sand and the fields and the playgrounds where kids were kids and boys were allowed to like girls. I was a child here once upon a time, long ago in the good old days. How scary. I'm only twenty-four.

I come home to Archer, who is quietly looking at books in the corner. He smiles, and a part of me feels responsible for all of this: all the change and the fear, because I chose to bring him into a

world where so much is unfair. A part of me wants to throw a temper tantrum and beg for my childhood to come back.

In my *day . . . I used to walk through fields to go to school—that was*
before they put the electric fences up. . . .

But tantrums are a waste of time, just like wishing for things
to change back to the way they were. And if I cannot undo the past,
I can at least do something about the future. I can help Archer seek
an even better place to view the ocean, a place that isn't PRIVATE and
blocked off and KEEP OUT. Because the beauty isn't all gone. It will
never be *all* gone. I hope.

Today Archer is nine months old. He has lived outside of me for
as long as I've carried him in my body, bouncing and kicking and
becoming human. Every day with him is an adventure, even as he
wriggles from my arms, resisting kisses with squints and squirms
and spit-up down the front of my shirt.

I have become as attached to him as one becomes to her limbs.
He's like an extra appendage—but more important than an arm or a
leg or even my head. Yes, I could easily live without arms and legs,
but without Archer? Not a chance.

I've become addicted to my child. I want to know where he is
at all times. I want to hear him breathing. I want to smell his hair.
When I spend afternoons without him, I am constantly checking
my pockets and purse, thinking maybe I have forgotten something.

Perhaps I lost an earring, or my sunglasses fell off without my knowing. I run around town like a madwoman so that I can come home and eat his nose and tickle his toes and hear that giggle. It's a cute nose, and I can't help myself sometimes. It's delicious.

Sometimes I remind myself of one of those overbearing aunties who kiss and cuddle and pinch the cheekies and speak with puckered lips and wide eyes and *Christ, I must look obnoxious.* But I'm obsessed with his smell and the way his cheeks feel against me and time will pass and soon I won't be able to kiss on him in public or anywhere for that matter, so I hold him close and gobble him up and then go back for seconds.

"I think I'm going through a phase," I tell my mother.

"That isn't a phase, I'm afraid," she says.

"What about now? Surely you don't miss the smell of my hair."

"Sometimes I do."

My mother may have held on to me as a baby, and maybe she's still holding on, but she has always been subtle in doing so, instilling in my brother, sister, and me a strong sense of self and independence and, most important, fearlessness. My normal childhood fears came out of *me*, not from worries fed to me by my parents. And I am very grateful for that.

When I was a child, I loved piñatas, except for the whole blindfold and spin part. I hated not seeing what I was trying to hit. I hated the idea that I would most likely swing and miss. I hated not being able to see what was in front of me, so I cheated.

I cheated until I could see. I had it down to a science. I would close both eyes until it came time to clobber the piñata with my baseball bat. Then I'd whack the shit out of the thing, with one eye wide-open, peeking. I'm pretty sure I wasn't the only one cheating at hitting the piñata as a child, that many and maybe even most children secretly peek out of their blindfolds so they can get a better swing at the candy-bellied beast. So they can see what they're doing, and do it well.

In order to make direct contact, Archer is going to have to see what he is swinging at. I want him to. The blindfold is an illusion, anyway. Everyone knows how easy it is to see through the threads in the cloth, to peek out from underneath.

≥ ⚘ ≤

I'm the new girl at the local mom group. I am here because it's time for me to get out of the house and expose Archer to babies his age. I put him down beside the other children, in front of a stack of toys he couldn't care less about. He squeezes his blankie and stares off into space.

"I will never let my daughter play with a Barbie."

"Barbies are awful. Just awful."

One of the anti-Barbie mommies turns to me. "I bet you're glad you have a son and don't have to deal with the filth that's out on shelves for little girls these days." Her shirt says "stay at home feminist" in lowercase type on the front.

I think for a moment. I remember Barbie well. I loved her, personally, but I say nothing.

Just nod and wave. Nod and wave.

"Speaking of inappropriate, I called the corporate office at Target the other day because *Maxim* magazine was at my daughter's eye level and, call me crazy, but shouldn't I be able to buy toilet paper without my daughter being bombarded by Christina Aguilera in a leather bikini?"

I want to tell her what I feel, that telling children to look away only makes them want to look more. That putting fig leaves on men's magazines isn't going to solve anything. It's only going to create more questions for parents to ignore. I am afraid that this woman is the same woman who will have boys suspended on the playground for kissing her daughter. *My* boy.

"I don't mind *Maxim* magazine," I say. The entire world is full of *Maxim* magazine. It's not going to disappear with a few phone calls to corporate offices." The women are silent. They look at each other and nod. *She just doesn't get it.*

I'm obviously getting off on the wrong foot. I'm here to make friends. I *need* to make friends.

"Never mind," I say, clearing my throat.

But it's too late, and I suddenly feel like I did in second grade, when the girl who was supposed to be my best friend paid the new girl her two-dollar lunch money to play with me, and how I heard the whole thing when I was in the bathroom, peeing with my feet up so no one would notice my white Keds and pink socks with the pom-poms on the heel. I'm on the outside of their little club. And they don't even know my name.

"I'm Rebecca."

I was told that "joining a mom group" was what "good mothers" do, and I listened. *Why did I listen?* I wish I could just be normal and enjoy the company of other mothers. I wish I could just sit among these women and laugh like them and whisper like them and talk about the statistics of rape victims on playgrounds without clenching my fists.

I take that back. I wouldn't wish that on my worst enemy: paranoia and the kind of fear that spreads like fire. I watch the flames rise and back away slowly, all the while wondering how these mothers expect their children to look both ways when they insist they wear bandanas over their eyes. I wonder how parents plan to educate their children with their fingers crossed behind their backs—the truth hidden away in locked boxes.

I know these women are good parents. They are doing their best, trying to protect their children from all the evil in the world. And I know worrying comes with the territory. I worry too. But sex isn't evil and dolls aren't the enemy and little boys who kiss girls on the playground aren't sexual predators. A child doesn't have to be afraid to be informed. I don't want to hear excuses for why mothers shoo boys from their daughters. Fear is the sword that separates us. Men from women. Woman from herself.

Who are we to tame our children before they even understand what it means to be wild? Who are we to limit their experience with our own closed minds? And don't we remember what it felt like to be kids? Because if I'm not mistaken, every single thing my mother told me not to do I did. Twice.

It isn't my job to blindfold, but it is my job to point in the right direction. Life is dirty and messy and sexy and half-naked sometimes, even within the great wall we have built up to the sky. Even with Bibles and seat belts and precautions. I don't want to lose sleep over being afraid. The blindfold has never interested me, and besides, it's far too easy to peek.

Taking Barbie away will not discourage a future eating disorder. It's not *Maxim* magazine's fault that children grow into sexual creatures who want to wear tube tops at twelve. It's our day and age. One cannot blindfold a child to what has saturated society. If we choose to breed today, then we must also choose to chill the fuck out. The world is not a terrible place. It is only a victim of bad publicity. Protection is our duty as parents, but fearlessness is our greatest gift.

Because no matter what happens, the only way for us to live unafraid is by learning how to live side by side with the monsters. We cannot run from them anymore. There just aren't as many hiding places as there used to be. There aren't as many rabbit holes and trees with leafy branches and tall grass fields and fairylands.

Ready or not, here we come. . . .

ONE YEAR,

a Retrospective

X

DEAR ARCHER,

A year ago today, you were born. . . .

At first I didn't think I was ready for you, but I was wrong. Determined to come into the world, you knocked several times without my hearing you. You may have rang the bell, but my hands were over my ears and I was singing "Lalala."

I touched my belly and felt you flicker. I knew you were faceless, a cluster of cells the size of a seed, and yet you had become me. You were more than a biological effect; you were a manifestation of a future unknown to both of us and all of us, and your presence was like a ripple upon the face of time, my skin and flesh. You were always inside of me, in a way. You were always in the back of my mind, quietly pacing like a gentleman.

On the day your father and I fell in love with you—your little spirit, possessing me with new life—I fell asleep, smiling, and dreamed for nine months.

I dreamed of you as a boy with big green eyes and as a girl with long blonde hair. I dreamed of giving birth to your father. I dreamed of giving birth to myself. I dreamed of unwrapping a globe with an unfamiliar topography, shape-shifting continents, the Rocky Mountains thrown upon the Greek Isles, rolling knolls superimposed on Death Valley.

I spoke to you and wrote letters, not yet knowing your name. Secrets and stories and the way I felt carrying you around with me, everywhere I went. A road trip to San Francisco with you inside me, just the two of us, and stopping in Big Sur to meditate, feet dangling from the bluffs, the farthest edge of the world. We had just found out about you then, so I quit smoking and chewed toothpicks and drove with my hair out the window and turned the music up loud enough for you to dance.

I felt you inside of me like divine inspiration. I wrote madly and touched my belly every time I had a decent thought. You were my muse before I saw your face on the ultrasound. Before they told me you were going to be a boy and I sobbed with excitement. Before we even knew your name.

We named you Archer for the strong man you would become and Sage for the thoughts in your tiny skull that might someday push for great change, or do good, or inspire a person or a place or a story. Perhaps every mother believes her child will do great things. Will be strong as a bowman, precise in his aim, graceful and brave—sage as the great prophets and thinkers and poets. Modern day Homers or Sapphos or Sartres . . . *or Archers*.

Months passed quickly, and then you were born.

In one year you have held up a mirror and taught me more about life than I imagined I could ever learn from an infant, a baby, and now a one-year-old. I look at you and see life. I see the good fun of dirt, because you throw up your hands full of filth and smile sheepishly. You are the love of my life. You humble me. I am a greater person because of you. You: Archer, the little boy with the marble eyes and the two front teeth.

Instead of feeling like more of a grownup, I feel like I am a little girl again, in pigtails, sneaking cookies from the jar. Unspooling yarn with you and jumping on the bed.

I never danced in the middle of the grocery store until I met you. I'd forgotten how to put flowers in my hair and play peekaboo behind every tree. I never fell face first into the sand and laughed for days. Thank you for that. Life is so much more fun dirty and messy than neat and tidy and boring.

I think if I were one year old, we would be best friends. I think I would enjoy shredding magazine pages with you and patting the dogs and swaying to the music and laughing at the squirrels as they chase each other across the sidewalk.

I got you, babe. Like an imaginary friend come to life, my little koala bear to eat off my plate and smear cake in my face and scratch my eyeballs out of my head.

Today we spent the day at the beach. Gammy and I built you your own little pool on the sand, and then, slowly, the tide washed it away, and you reached your arms up to me and I pulled you from the foam. This is what being your mother for the past year has been like for me—protecting you when I can, building walls around you, knowing they will fall, digging pools in the sand with wind in my eyes and sand in my butt and again when the pools dry and disappear, me on my knees digging away.

I am now the self who, fully clothed, is happy to play in the sand with rocks in my hair, happy to soak myself and build drip castles that become erased in time. The self who chafes and freezes and *whatever it takes to make you smile.*

The beach is vast. The ocean is dangerous, so here, let me build you another little pool and we will sit in it together and watch the sea, side by side, splashing away with our bare feet until you are old enough to walk away and swim with sharks and do handstands in the surf. I get to sleep with you tonight because we're at Gammy and Papa's house, and as I type, you are waiting for me with your eyebrows up and your hands over your head.

Years from now, when you read this and all of the letters I have written you, I imagine you will put your hands over your ears and sing "Lalala," but for now I'll keep writing them because they help me remember all the moments and feelings that get lost in the quickness of life and watching you grow. Because you are growing so fast. I know that what they say is true: I will blink, and you will be a little boy. And a teenager. And then a man.

Whoever you decide to become, I know there are a great many seeds of goodness inside of you. That if I do my job well enough, those seeds will grow steadily and, over time, become a great tree. I am also well aware that one day you will outgrow our garden and uproot yourself to be planted again within the great wood of the unknown.

But I mustn't dwell on that, even if I get carried away sometimes with the quickness of this past year and how everything changes in an instant. You are here with me now. In my arms. One year old. Thank you for choosing me to mother you. Thank you for sneaking in through my window and saying "Boo! Here I am!" Thank you for stirring and purring and screaming and crying and laughing and talking and standing and jumping. You are my exclamation point in a world of dot-dot-dots. You are my star in a sky muted by city lights. You are my sun. My son. My sun.

Love, Mommy

UNDER
the Affluence

IT'S THE FIRST DAY of summer and Archer and I are rolling around in the sand at our local park. Spanish-speaking nannies
crowd around the same edge of the sandbox day after day. They
chat among themselves and pass shovels and Pirate's Booty to the
children. Archer and I find a shady spot, roomy enough for the two
of us and our bag of sand toys, and start working on a proper hole
in which to bury our bare feet.

I try to eavesdrop, but my three years of high school *español*
did little to hone my ability to understand anything besides talk of
school supplies and bodily functions.

Tengo un lápiz.

¿Donde está la biblioteca?

¿Puedo ir al baño?

If anyone feels the need to strike up a conversation about
libraries or bathrooms, I'll be prepared.

A woman with three children shows up, her three nannies trailing behind her, an entourage of offspring and hired help. I watch them with spite—jealous that there are mothers who can afford to stay home with their kids *and* have help. Lots of help. The mother lifts a paperback book to her face and eyes me over the pages.

She knows I am watching her.

I look away.

I hide my chipped nails behind me and lift my head. I am as image conscious as the next person and think, smugly, *Even if I could afford to hire a nanny, I wouldn't. A mother should be with her children, like mine was with me.* This isn't true of course, but here I am, lying to myself in order to justify my afternoons of swing sets and strolls, as jealous women so often do.

It's hard not to judge her. It is hard to be broke in a neighborhood of affluence, and even though I am happy to be at home with Archer, I am envious that we cannot afford the luxuries of the other women in the neighborhood. The proverbial Joneses are around every corner, pushing their accessorized Bugaboos with perfectly manicured hands and precious stones like boulders on their fingers.

Archer is just beginning to crawl when many of his peers are walking, and I wish I could be like him and not care. I wish I could be happy crawling around amongst the mothers who are miles ahead of me, sprinting toward the finish line.

A little boy takes Archer's shovel and runs off, and I open my mouth to say something, but nothing comes out. What would be the point? Archer is perfectly content combing the sand with his fingers. I follow him on all fours toward the swing set.

It's a perfect Los Angeles day, and pushing Archer back and forth on the swing in Van Ness Park fills me with love for a place I am usually quick to complain about. The sky is full of cotton animals and the wind blows through my hair and Archer makes clucking sounds as he rocks back and forth, smiling at three dogs fetching balls on the other side of the fence.

I wasn't planning on raising a child in Los Angeles. Hollywood is not exactly the place people bring their families to settle down. And like everyone else who ended up in this twisted Mecca of addiction and narcissism, I moved here for a dream: to try and be somebody.

Los Angeles has a way of penetrating even the thickest skins and tricking people into thinking they want most of all to be famous. Wanting to be somebody, as opposed to wanting *to do something*. That is what drives Hollywood. Like a leggy blonde phoenix rising from the turn-of-the-century dust balls, the streets of Los Angeles were paved by attention-seekers, even if they didn't know they were attention-seekers yet.

More than once I have been asked if I would be interested in putting Archer in commercials. Television. "The kid could do movies, he really could." And every time I have said, "No! Absolutely not!" there was a part of me that wanted to say, "Yes! Wow! Thanks for asking!"

It is said that Los Angeles a city of fakers and posers. Maybe. But it is also a collective example of what happens when too many people are honest. Brutally honest. And perhaps that is why it is so scary. We all want recognition. We all want to be beautiful and wealthy. Here, we are failures if we are not. And so I struggle with what it means to say no, a word relatively new to my vocabulary.

It is a strange feeling to want to protect my child from the things I came here for. And it makes me think maybe we should be elsewhere instead. So much temptation. It's far too easy to be romanced by devils with plastic wings. They look so big and white and real.

I grew up in the suburbs. Does it show? Will it be obvious that Archer grew up smack-dab in the middle of Hollywood, spitting distance from Paramount Studios? A view of the Hollywood sign from his nursery windows? Surrounded by agents and actors and producers on a street blocked off to through traffic for filming? Half of the children his age already have agents and are booking jobs at six months. I know it isn't the norm anywhere else. But it's so easy to forget when it's all you know.

When I met Hal I was trying to decide between moving to New York City or Morocco to join the Peace Corps. I had been in Los Angeles for five years and I was ready to inhale something other than Hummer fumes. Gypsy cab fumes, for instance. Or camel fumes. It didn't matter to me. I just wanted out.

And sometimes I still do. There are days when I fantasize about leaving. To Portland or Seattle or San Francisco. New York or London or the Galápagos Islands. All places probably better suited for raising Archer, somewhere rich in culture and thought, where actors are what you see when you turn on the television instead of all you see when you walk down the street.

It's hard to establish some kind of home when part of you wants out; to root yourself when all of your instincts are telling you to uproot. But we are here. In Los Angeles. Where palm trees are carefully placed and planted and we are made to think they grow wild. Where people are carefully chosen for sinister reasons and we are made to think they "made it" based on talent and perseverance. The question is, will this factor into Archer's existence? Will the agents and the child actors and the Angeleno culture brainwash him into thinking the Hollywood sign is more than just what's left over from Hollywoodland? Is it naive to think that I can stop it? That I can somehow reverse the smoke so that he cannot inhale its fumes?

Archer wipes his eyes and starts to yawn, so I figure it's time to call it a day. We have one whole toy left after being robbed by the other children, who clutch shovels and rakes with Archer's name smeared upon them in Sharpie marker. I politely ask around the circle if we can *por favor* have our rake back.

"Hola. ¿Donde estás un bucket y rake y shovel y truck y autóbus y baño y papel y sand funnel thing y agua bottle?"

My horrible effort at Spanish seems to be mysteriously earning the respect of the nannies. They introduce themselves to me one by one and ask if I am new. I'm not quite sure what "new" means, but I answer with a nod and a *"¡Sí, gracias!"*

I introduce the nannies to Archer, *"mi hermano,"* which is unfortunate, because *hermano* means brother, not son. I laugh, embarrassed, waving as we slip out the gate toward home.

We don't get far before I hear one of the nannies calling after me, her double stroller in tow and a third child in her arms. Her eyes are round and intense, her single thick braid exuding a strength and pragmatism that feels suddenly intimidating to me. The children hanging off of her are angelic, and she balances them with ease and confidence.

"Rebecca . . . " she says, and I wonder how she knows my name.

She looks around before glaring at me. "You are nanny?" she whispers.

"Um . . . no."

"You have a nanny?"

"No."

"Just you?"

"Just me."

"You need a nanny then."

"Not right now, thank you."

"I see. Well, maybe not yet, but you will. You can't do it all yourself. You need nanny? I find you nanny. I am Maria, and I can find you nanny anytime."

"O . . . kay. I'll remember that, thank you."

"I am here every day, in the shaded corner by the swing set. Just find me when you're ready."

"*Gracias.*"

"*Habla español?*"

"*Sí. Un poco.*"

"*¡Nosotras queres taemos guatalastar cuando jurestamo si genesta moralas todos y esta malagualqufinal!*"

I have no idea what she is saying, but it sounds extremely *importante*. The nanny pimp is speaking code for sure. Either that or it is just really advanced Spanish. Spanish 5, maybe. I only got to Spanish 3.

I look at her hopelessly. She pats me on the back, nods her head, and checks the palm trees for spies.

"We talk next time," she says before disappearing into a gated mansion. "*Adiós* Archer."

I push on toward home, daydreaming about how it would be if I had a nanny. I imagine myself making to-do lists and wrapping sandwiches in the fridge. My heart jumps at the thought of quiet afternoons at the coffee shop, finishing my novel, headphones securely over my ears, calling to check on Archer from the graffitied bathroom at Insomnia Café. My fantasies take on a life of their own until soon I am the exact same woman I rolled my eyes at in the sandbox.

Envy is a funny thing: a refuge for denial and hope, a dangerous kind of frustration reserved for people like me who don't understand why it has to be so hard. Why overnight success can't just happen. *Why isn't there money falling from the sky onto my face?* I think. *Why does time have to pass so quickly? Why haven't any of my birthday wishes come true?*

I take the long way home, down 1st Street through Hancock Park, each multimillion-dollar mansion more beautiful than the next. We pass my dream house, with its glass office on the second floor and the ivy that spreads across the doors, searching for a way inside.

I peek through the slits in the fence. A vacant swing set sways slightly on the impeccably kept lawn, and white roses frame a patio with a fire pit and chairs made of hollowed-out trees. I can't help myself. I must peek through the cracks of "what if" whenever I pass by.

Larchmont Boulevard is bustling, crowded with strollers and suits on Bluetooth earpieces making deals and collecting their Peet's coffee or their Coffee Bean or Starbucks. I quietly curse what has happened to the "small-town feel" as I order my grande soy latte.

Every day the same woman sets up shop outside, her back against the glass window beside her son. She's beautiful and tall and carries with her a plastic case of beads and string and little clasps that look like hands. Glass and wood and crystal beads with little faces. She doesn't make eye contact with anyone but her boy. She sits outside by the window with her coffee and materials, sometimes for hours, as her son peels at straws and kicks the window with his scuffed shoes. The woman works through the morning with squinty eyes and rocks her son's stroller with her right foot. Back and forth and back and forth. She could probably work at home, but she must like it here at the coffee shop, with her table in the shade out on the sidewalk.

I pass her, walking behind two women pushing strollers—both mothers like me, mothers like the woman with the beads and the stroller she drags back and forth with her foot.

"It's like torture what she does to that child," one woman says to the other.

"I know it. Her poor son just sits there all day waiting for her to finish."

"It's so sad what some children have to go through."

"She doesn't even pay attention to him. She just sits there and makes crappy jewelry all day. . . . "

I want to turn around and say hello to the woman with her Caboodle full of beads, but I don't. I want to tell her that I identify with her—rocking her son to sleep as she strings beads on fishing wire, concentrating on the two things in her life that will never be less than inspired and inspiring: her child and her craft—working and creating and mothering all at once. Because she has to. Because maybe she wants to stand on her own two feet without locking her knees. Because she bought that coffee with the money she made selling a box full of bracelets, staining the coffee lid with lipstick she forgot she even had on.

I take a closer look at her cup and see my name. And the lipstick stain looks just like mine. She is no different from the women who mock her or the mother with her trail of nannies or the mother who keeps an immaculate rose garden or even me. She is doing what she has to—balancing her worlds, her loves, her selves.

We are separated only by circumstance. The rich from the poor, the single mother from the stay-at-home wife. It is impossible to see the mirrors in the broken glass after the stones have been thrown. I know this only because I throw them too. I throw them quietly in my head or out loud, eyes pressed against the holes of other people's destinies. I throw them when I pretend that I am different or better or entitled.

The grass may be greener on the other side of the boulevard, but it's never going to change. Because whatever "it" is will never be enough. Not for the mama who strings beaded necklaces at the café or the mother with three nannies at the park or the family who dines where the ivy cannot reach. We are all victims of our own misdiagnosis and slaves to the holes we peek through.

Archer makes eyes at a passing toddler in a shiny new Bugaboo stroller. He pulls his pacifier out of his mouth and throws it over his head into the gutter, as if to say, "Pacifier? What pacifier? I don't need a pacifier." He does this when he is confronted by other children, trying to blend with the crowd in his way. I pick it up, wipe it off, and put it in my pocket, knowing as soon as we are out of eye range from Bugaboo and baby, Archer will want it again.

We wait at the crosswalk for our right-of-way. Cars roll to a stop, and we drop off the curb onto the street, making our way across the intersection, toward the blinking red hand.

And by the time we reach the other side of Beverly, Archer is sucking his pacifier again.

BURPING CONTESTS
and Stationary Bikes

HAL IS IN THE KITCHEN and I am on my computer. The light on the baby monitor is bouncing and we both look away. I'm trying to concentrate on my work, while Hal takes a break from the script he's working on to finish the dishes. We aren't speaking. My eyes are swollen from crying and Hal puts down a clean plate and rests his head in his hands.

"I feel trapped," I say.

"I feel alone," he says back.

And our silence is so much louder than Archer's cries from the back room, which we ignore together, something we agree to do without speaking a word.

I don't even remember how our fight started. I just remember how it ended. With me hyperventilating, tearing at my eyes, wanting to run away. With Hal stomping off down the hall. With Archer wide awake and crying.

Ever since Archer was born, any sign of turmoil between his father and me upsets him. It's like he has this secret power that causes him to be psychic during the precise times I wish he wouldn't be. Whenever Hal and I argue, or when I feel overwhelmed and break down, Archer cries too. He feels my tears against him and starts wailing.

"Are you going to get him?" I finally ask.

"Are you?"

"He has been crying for almost twenty minutes."

"Does that mean you want me to get him?"

"No," I say, "I will."

I storm down the hall and open Archer's bedroom door. He stands and motions to his red blankie and pacifier on the ground. He throws them out of his crib when he's angry, casting his bait, hoping he might catch me or his father with his trickery.

He's caught me. I'm too tired not to quiet him with kisses. I'm too lonely not to pick him up and hold him and hug him. We stand in his bedroom, in the darkness for several seconds, rocking back and forth to The Innocence Mission's "Now the Day Is Over," which plays for Archer on repeat every night while he sleeps.

I hum along to the song, and Archer nuzzles into my shoulder with his little red blankie. Two drifters! / Off to see the world. / There's such a lot of world to see. The song reminds me of taking the train across Scotland when I was nineteen. I made a traveler's mix, a collection of songs about vagabonds and explorers, and "Moon River" was on it. Cheesy, perhaps, but I've always had a soft spot for Henry Mancini and his nostalgic riffs, especially during times like this when I just want the darkness to cradle me in its cold hands. Times like that summer five years ago when I chased trains across Europe, trying to find myself, studying the countryside and cityscape from the windows of the Eurostar, seducing myself with a homemade soundtrack.

I turn down the stereo and carry Archer into the harsh light of the living room, sticking my tongue out at the back of Hal's head as I take a seat with Archer on my lap. I say nothing. The wall between us seems to have grown taller and thicker since I plucked Archer from his crib, since our silence went on interrupted. A part of me wishes Archer would cry again so I could have something else to keep me occupied besides all of these thoughts of anger and loneliness. The lights on the monitor continue to flash and flicker, even though Archer isn't crying anymore. I guess it's because I forgot to turn the music off in his bedroom.

I know that married couples fight, especially married couples with children. But my parents didn't, not in front of us anyway. And if we did overhear them arguing, it ended quickly. Maybe, then, I have a false sense of reality, because there were no parents on laptop computers when I was a little girl. No fathers writing screenplays or mothers writing books, and maybe that was a good thing. Maybe my parents weren't always distracted like we are, listening to each other's muffled speech through the headphones we wear while we are working. Whatever it is that is tearing us apart, I feel like a failure. I feel like I suck at marriage.

It's our work that's coming between us, I think. It feels like we have nothing in common besides the son we made together. And though we sleep together side by side, our legs tangled and hands touching, our thoughts are on ourselves, focused on our own individual worlds and what we need to do to realize our dreams.

Hal pretends like he is madly working, but I know he isn't. The sound he makes with the keys is too rhythmic. He's playing solitaire again, a game I never learned how to play.

I wrap Archer's blanket around him and whisper "I love you" in his ear, and I wonder if he would hate me if I left his father. If we left each other. We don't talk about that when we fight, but in my head I keep thinking, *What if I just walked out the door?*

I lie down on the couch and turn on *Sesame Street* and Archer curls up on my chest and we stay like that, just the two of us, until we fall asleep.

The next morning I go to the gym early and ride the stationary bike for forty minutes. I bike seven whole miles, even though I haven't moved. I always find it strange, the idea that somehow I am traveling miles and miles without moving from this spot. *An easy metaphor,* I think. *Too easy.*

I think about how it all began with Hal and me. It wasn't even that long ago, and yet here we are. Somehow we traveled the span of a hundred miles in the time it takes most to go seven, both of us footsore and cramped from running these past two years.

≥ ⚘ ≤

Two years ago, I was meeting a friend for coffee on Melrose when Hal showed up. Our friend thought we would make good work partners for a pilot about kids from the suburbs who wanted to start a garage band. I told Hal I liked his idea, and he clapped his hands and said, "Yes!"

Van Halen was playing a little too loud for a coffee shop but not loud enough for a coffee shop on Melrose, where music perpetually blasts from the boutiques, the bass bumping loud enough to trip its tourist patrons. It was my first time there. Hal's too.

"I hear you can smoke here after 6:00 PM," he told me.

He lit my cigarette at 5:59.

At first it was just about work. Hal and I got together almost daily to do research, watching movies and DVDs of *My So-Called Life*, my favorite television show of all time. I tried to impress him with my knowledge of music, except it was the wrong kind of knowledge. The only bands we had in common were the Misfits and the Smiths, so he played "Some Girls Are Bigger Than Others" and "Die, Die, Die My Darling" on his guitar, and I sang along, trying to hide my burgeoning crush.

One night, during the Broiler Room episode of *My So-Called*

Life, our hands touched, and suddenly I was twelve years old again, salvaging what willpower I had left to keep myself from pinning him down and sticking my tongue down his throat. I let my hand stay like that through the entire episode, trying to manage my swallowing as Jordan Catalano pressed his flannel-wearing self against Angela Chase. Eventually the show ended, and I went home.

I chased Hal like a dog after that. I brought him lunch and watched him play guitar in his garage until 3:00 AM, even when I had an early work day the next morning. And when he picked me up one night and opened the door for me, even though we were only friends, I knew it wouldn't be long. I called him and text-messaged him dirty notes until finally he called. At 3:30 in the morning on a Thursday. I came over, even though I knew it was against every rule in the dating book. I didn't care. I just wanted to be close to him, and we smoked cigarettes by the pool in his backyard until he finally kissed me. I had been waiting an hour for that kiss. And before that, days, weeks . . . maybe even forever.

"This was supposed to be a work partnership," he said.

"Oh well."

We crept past Hal's roommates, who were passed out on the couch, and went to his room, and I waited until the lights were off before I got into bed next to him.

Every day after that I came over to find him on his back by the pool, tanned in his torn swim trunks, with his guitar in the shade. And because he had no money, he took me on dates to the ninety-nine-cent store, where we would buy malt liquor and bootleg DVDs of old sitcoms, and it was perfect. We were like children playing in the grass and staining our jeans and getting soaked by the sprinklers with the dogs wrestling for our attention when all we could see was each other. Sometimes I would catch him looking at me and he would catch me looking at him, and even though we couldn't see the stars when we cuddled together outside at night, we looked for them anyway. We went swimming and kissed in the shallow end and floated around on rafts and wondered how it would all end.

Because it always ends, doesn't it?

Maybe, I remember thinking, hoping that the rain wouldn't come and wash away our months of mildewed rafts and Captain Morgan. I crossed my fingers that the changing seasons wouldn't change our hearts.

The tan has since disappeared and the pool has been replaced with a blow-up version that neither Hal nor I can fit into. And all those long nights of staying awake so that I wouldn't accidentally fart in my sleep in front of him have been replaced with farting contests that I usually win.

It always ends, doesn't it?

Maybe.

When I come home, Hal is at the piano with Archer on his lap. Archer is banging away at the keys and Hal keeps on singing, and suddenly whatever seemed so terrible last night doesn't seem so bad. *These are my people,* I think, and my carefully made plans to leave fall apart. Just like they always do when I come home and see Hal as he really is. The man I stalked two summers ago. The man who makes me laugh and Archer smile and fills our home with music. And suddenly there is no place in the world I would rather be.

And then I remember how when I first met Hal I knew he would be the father of my child. I had a flash several weeks after we met, when I came over for a BBQ and he answered the door with a friend's daughter on his shoulders, and I just knew. Perhaps it was just wishful thinking, but I like to think that there was a reason for our meeting at the coffee shop that afternoon, and a reason we had Archer together.

I sit down beside Hal and Archer and try my best to sing along. We are a family now, and it's not supposed to be easy and no one can be happy all the time and there will be plenty of days when one or even both of us will be standing in the doorway, on the other side of the music. And that's okay too. As long as we all hold on to our keys and know how to find our way home.

I want Hal to be around as Archer grows up, just like my dad was for me. And I want to be there to watch. I want to come home and see Archer on Hal's shoulders. I want us to be a family.

Hal stops playing piano and turns to me.

"While you were gone Archer pooped the biggest poop I've ever seen."

"Really? Like how big exactly."

"It was like a dinosaur egg, I swear."

"Did you take a picture?"

"No. I couldn't find my camera."

"You should have used the one on your phone."

And just like that, everything is back to normal. The fight is over. Neither of us has won, and it doesn't matter, because Archer has laid a dinosaur poop egg.

Maybe Archer will be the glue that holds us together, because sometimes love isn't enough. Sometimes it's more complicated than that. And that's okay. Because more than anything, Archer is our overlapping circle in the Venn diagram. He is what matters most to us, after all, so maybe it's not so bad that he keeps us from throwing each other out on the street.

"You okay?"

"Yeah, you?"

"Yeah."

We hug each other for a long time, with Archer in between us. On the piano bench, banging away.

"I don't really feel trapped," I say.

"I only feel alone sometimes," Hal says back.

Archer burps and we laugh. Hal burps next, and if I could burp on cue I'd follow suit, but I was never able to do that. *Thought that counts.*

The days of courtship and make-out sessions have been replaced by burping contests, but maybe that isn't such a bad thing. Because eventually, in every intimate relationship, *it* happens. You go from wearing makeup to bed to not wearing makeup at all. From talking dirty in bed to *really* talking dirty—about yellow poop and gas and ingrown hairs.

Marriage isn't about genetic perfection. It's is about the half-eaten cake in the fridge. "I made it for you, but then I got hungry." It's about the late-night snack runs, even if they're the wrong kind of snacks. It's about trying. And messing up. And falling down. And getting up. And making up. And riding the stationary bike, sometimes for long periods of time. Marriage is about the flowers that grow wild in the sidewalk cracks, often disguised as weeds and equally hard to manage. Blooming year-round, with wishes to blow against the wind if you believe. And I do. I believe. Even if I kick the sidewalk sometimes.

I am willing to trade the fragrance of "romance" for the stench of dirty feet. For cookie crumbs in bed. And that's love, man. Smelling each other's less-than-pleasant fumes and giggling in bed until 4:00 AM. Gaining weight. Getting older. None of that matters. *Who cares? It's just me.*

Strip away the mask. Remove the black lace panty set. The makeup. The various deodorizers. Marriage is what happens the morning after—hungover and bloated, without makeup. Gone are the roses, perhaps. But the dandelions remain, quietly growing in the cracks.

RIGHT BEHIND

ॐ

HE CAN SAY "PERCH." And "anemone." He can say "horse" and "carriage" and "Ferrari" and "Salvador Ferragamo." He can also say, "I feel like a dinner roll," except he doesn't say any of these things in English. He speaks entirely in his own language, babbling as if we should be able to understand him. As if *we're* the ones with issues, the ones who are *behind*.

"Archer! How was your day?"

"Goo dit. Di gah la pooduplaaaaaah gigi! Alalalawalawala-walala. *Hooooot!*"

"Yes! Dit! Dit you have fun?"

"Orteetatick."

"Fantastic! Shall we read a book?"

"Plth. Jow. Jow in lapalapa."

"Good boy with your words, Arch! My lapalapa is right! Come sit down in my lapalapa and we will jow pth!"

"Garlo ifkis bahbahbahlooooooo. Couscous."

"*Yes!* Good boy! That's right! We're going to read *Ten Little Dinosaurs!* Can you say dinosaur?"

"Golinrarar. Dit doot dit loop."

"Yes! Good! We're going to go to the park! Can you say sandbox?"

"No!"

"Come on, dude! *Saaaaandbox.*"

"Garsjklaks! Lucalalciallica."

"Good man!!!!" I say, anxiously waiting for real words to get mixed in with the gibberish.

Did he say Lucite? That's a word!

It's like trying to find the 3-D picture in those digital prints with all the multicolored dots. I stare and I stare and I tell everyone I can see the picture.

"It's a palm tree!" I say.

But really, I can't see anything. Just a mixed-up rainbow of unknown pictures.

I would love to understand *something*. One word would be nice. "Mama," maybe? My first word was "shampoo," so I point at the bottle in the bathtub.

"Shampoo!" I say, because you never know. Maybe shampoo will be his first word too.

I point at the fish beyond the glass that curves over us, full of water and kelp, and Archer makes the *oooooh* sound before kicking to be put down. He's approaching seventeen months and still isn't walking and has no desire, it seems, to try. He is happy as he is, crawling swiftly between the legs of strangers, and I'm okay with that. Or, I would be if everywhere we went people weren't so set on telling us what we're doing wrong.

Archer is behind schedule, and apparently I'm supposed to be training him so that he can do all of the things kids his age are supposed to be doing. Like talking and walking and finding a cure for cancer.

He crawls toward the strip of sun that peeks through the opening of the door, seducing him with its light. A man with two small children eyes us from across the hall. Both children look younger than Archer and are walking, pointing at the fish and saying, "Look, Daddy." I'm not surprised when the man approaches us and volunteers to help teach Archer how to walk.

"Is this your son?" he asks.

I nod and follow after Archer, who is pushing open the door with his head.

"He's not walking yet?" The man gives me a look like I'm crazy. "Have you tried teaching him?" he asks.

If I ignore him, maybe he will go away, I think. But he doesn't go away. They never do.

"I taught my twins how to walk when they were eleven months old," he brags.

Can't you see we're trying to chase the light? Can't you see we're perfectly content doing our own thing? Can't you see that he's a baby?

"Aw, come on, little man!" he grins, ignoring me while he leaves his children to wander aimlessly beside the sharks. He pushes by me and grabs Archer by the hands and stands him on his feet.

"Like this!" he says. "You teach him by walking him around like this."

"That's okay," I say, picking Archer up. "I'll take it from here."

In a daze of frustration and doubt, I carry Archer outside to the tide pools and then in circles. I know he is behind schedule. I know he's supposed to be talking by now. My pediatrician has reminded me twice.

"Is he saying words yet?"

"No. I mean, yeah. I mean, kinda."

"Kinda?"

"He said 'dragon' once and he says 'Mama' and 'no.'"

But that was kind of a lie. What kind of mother lies to her pediatrician? I do. I lie. I don't know what else to do. I go back and forth between my selves, battling insecurity with faith:

Nothing is wrong with Archer.

But what if there is?

Don't worry so much!

He could have a developmental problem, and it could be all your fault!

That's insane. He's perfectly normal.

Maybe you're in denial. Maybe there is something seriously wrong with him and you're just sitting there looking the other way.

I'm looking at him! And he looks fine.

But is he?

Of course he is.

Yeah, well . . .

I spend the rest of the day at the aquarium trying to ennunciate the names of the animals.

"C-rrrrrrr-ah-bbbbbbb."

"Sea-hoooooorse."

"Hah-mer-head shaark."

Archer isn't paying attention to me though. He's too busy tracing the suction cups of snails over the glass and giggling. He's too busy enjoying himself. Living. Being in the moment, and to hell with what anyone says. Even me.

I wait for the man to be as far out of sight as possible before I pull Archer up on his feet and guide him toward the aquarium exit.

"Come on, Arch. Please. For me?"

But he screams. He doesn't want to walk. He wants to crawl.

And I don't know what to do, even though a part of me is envious of Archer's blatant disregard for anything I or anyone else tries to teach him or tell him to do. He doesn't care that he is the only child at the park who crawls to the swings or doesn't speak. He just smiles and waves at the helicopters. He laughs and kicks the wind with his feet.

"He's different," I hear myself saying out loud, my excuse for his lateness. I mask my fear with confidence.

"Einstein didn't speak in complete sentences until he was four, so *really* the whole Baby Einstein brand is totally off. The *real* Baby Einstein was like Archer—late and spacey."

I remind the world that Archer is genetically designed to be a genius.

"Did you know Archer's uncle is getting his PhD at Harvard, and his grandfathers both have their doctorates? Yeah. Mmmm-hmm. But Archer will most likely grow up to be a famous architect like his great-great-great-grandfather Frank Lloyd Wright."

It is only half-true, of course. The late Mr. Wright was my grandfather's grandfather by marriage, but no one needs to know that.

The thing is, none of these strangers really care that Archer is late. No one loses sleep over his lack of words, his crawling down the street while other kids his age are running. Skipping, even. No one cares but me. Not even the father of the twins at the aquarium. He'll go home and forget he ever ran into us. He won't even remember Archer's name or what I look like. But me? I'll remember every damn pore on his bulbous nose because I don't want to. Because I'm obsessed with doubting myself. Maybe I'm insecure and scared that I'm doing something wrong. Maybe my pride and "Screw the man" and "Fuck the book" has been the safest way to protect my naivete. Maybe I should have read a book. Maybe I should have done my homework like everybody else. Maybe instinct isn't enough.

I often care far too much what people think. But Archer does what he does for himself. His time. His place. His world. And during a time when children are expected to follow a set pattern in their development, it's a bit of a relief that he exists on his own watch. *I have a lot to learn from him,* I think.

I want to nurture his uniqueness. I want him to know that life is long, that he has plenty of time to walk and talk and follow the rules. I want him to grow up naturally, without a leash or a deadline, at least until he's old enough to understand his responsibilities.

But I also don't want him to fall behind. I am afraid of the consequences of his quirks. I have worn both types of shoes, the high heels and high-tops, and believe it or not, the heels were far more comfortable.

⇒ ❊ ⇐

"You love them no matter what. You love them through all of it. You persevere. You make it work. You do what you can."

These are the wise words spoken to me by the parent of one of the children I work with. The kids I chat with are sick—some terminal, some chronically. Some are born with cystic fibrosis or chromosomal abnormalities. Some have the dreaded "A" word. *Autism.*

Over the last three years, surrounded by children who suffer from one or several chronic maladies, I have had the opportunity to learn that health is not something you take for granted. I am grateful every day that Archer is a healthy child, not thinking for a second he could be anything but "normal," even though I am reminded daily that "normal" has nothing to do with anything at all. "Normal" is a word that shouldn't even exist.

I have asked myself repeatedly what I would do if Archer was sick, because although it is so apparent to me that the children weakest in health are strongest in spirit, it is still hard to grasp the possibility that my child may be different, "special," a word used to hide the fact that we are afraid. A word *I* use to hide the fact that *I* am afraid.

I catch Archer standing in the hall between the bathroom and the kitchen. He's unassisted and alone and so strikingly tall. I feel as if I'm trying to corner and approach a wild rabbit. I try not to act too excited as not to frighten him or make it seem like anything is out of the ordinary.

"Hey dude. What are you doing?"

My heart is pounding. *Oh my god,* I think. *He's walking. He's going to walk!*

Archer smiles and I get down on my knees and open my arms.

"Can you walk to me?"

Archer laughs. "Gaaaaaaaawaaaa. *Gaaaaawawawa!*" he says before dropping to his knees and crawling full steam toward the living room.

So close.

Next time, I think. *Definitely next time.*

I know how to be a friend to the children in the chat room. I play games and talk and say goodnight. On the other side of my pink font I crack jokes and give boy advice and hire the virtual DJs at our virtual dance parties. And though I say "I love you" every night before I sign off, I cannot look at the children in the face. I cannot hug them. I don't know how they smell or feel or what they look like dancing or crawling across the sidewalk, dragging their soft-soled shoes through the dirt. I am not their mother.

There is no reason to be afraid, they tell me.

There is nothing to be afraid of, I tell myself.

And I know in my heart this is true. I know that life doesn't give us anything we cannot handle.

Everything's going to be okay.

Everything's going to be okay.

And just like that, I come together. The fearful and the fearless. I repeat to myself what I already know, what I have known since Archer was born and our wet eyes met for the first time.

"I will love you no matter what. I will do what I can for you."

"Ooooooh! Aloooooooalaaaaaaloooo!" he says back.

And then, as if there were never a question, he stands up again and, smiling, walks straight into my arms.

I don't know if we're out of the woods yet, or what it even means to be *in* the woods. I don't even know what the trees are supposed to look like. No parent does. This is a dirt road we're all stumbling upon, muddy when it rains, dry and dusty in the heat. But dirt roads can be managed. They change. Everything does.

MISFITS

WHAT HAPPENS IN VEGAS stays in Vegas, unless nothing happens—nothing of any real consequence, anyway.

One of my earliest Vegas memories involves a foreign stranger, a broken boot heel, a pair of handcuffs, and a missing key. Nothing like being escorted out of the casino restroom by a security guard and a locksmith to get the party started.

Ah, yes. Those were the days.

Okay, so not really. Unless you consider being sawed out of a pair of cuffs half-naked as "good times." In the days before marriage and motherhood, Vegas was a common escape for my friends and me, who, when tired of our local strip (Sunset) fled to the only strip that didn't close at 2:00 AM—the strip that never closes. Nights became mornings. Clubs shape-shifted into seedy after-hours joints where we emerged as footsore drunks walking home in our party dresses in the harsh daylight. Of course, months later, we would all pile in the car to do it again.

I haven't been to Las Vegas since Hal and I married and, memorable as it was, it was hardly a party weekend. And just as I went from single to bride all those months ago, I have come full circle, back to Vegas for a bachelorette party weekend in honor of one of my oldest friends.

I tighten the straps on my bra so my boobs look bigger. It doesn't take much to turn a rack into a *rack*. I adjust, lift, pull, and push out and voila. Vegas ready!

"Can you see my ass when I bend over?"

"Just a little bit."

"Perfect."

This is my first time away from Archer, and I plan to make it worth my while. I don't have a curfew or a babysitter to relieve from her duties. I don't even know what time it is, and that's just fine with me, I think.

Don't think! Keep applying eye shadow, and don't think!

So I don't. I apply double the makeup and spritz an extra spray of perfume under my arms. I pack my ID and cash in an old clutch bag and find, as I do, an accidental time capsule of broken cigarettes and old ticket stubs: Azure Ray at The Troubadour and the New Pornographers at The Wiltern. I shake out the dried tobacco over the toilet, but I can't bear to throw away the faded stubs. I safely place them in the secret front pocket of my bag, and *ziiiiip*.

"Everyone ready?"

I leave our hotel room satisfied with my ensemble, excited by the night ahead. *Rawr.*

"Let's go get trashed! Wooooooo!"

"Yeeeeeeeiiiii!"

And we do. We make friends with a bunch of single guys who have a reserved booth and plenty of bottles. Bottles they let us drink in exchange for our presence. It's a trade everyone is happy with. We get to drink for free. They get crotch-shots from drunk chicks with penis necklaces. Everybody wins.

The bride-to-be takes the stage with her penis veil, and I dance until my feet bleed and my shoes are stained with vodka from spilled martinis.

The DJ shouts "last call," and the lights in the club flicker. But instead of following my friends out after-hours, I go back to the hotel. I don't want the sun to reveal the truth: That I'm a big faker—hiding behind my little black dress and red suede ankle boots, howling and hollering with my hands in the air, my wedding ring back at the hotel.

I used to be able to party all night long, wake up at noon, and then do it again. So what happened? Parenthood? Old age? Am I twenty-five going on forty?

"I'll know it's time to go home when I start showing strangers photos of my kids," my friend's sister explained over breakfast yesterday morning, and now I think I know what she meant.

I think of what has changed since the last time I was here, at this exact same hotel. The birth of my son. The beginning of a new life. And in the reflection of the elevator's mirrored glass, I hardly recognize myself.

I slide open the door to my room and confront an explosion of clothes and makeup and camera cases. I remove my shoes and wipe the blush off my face. I'm glad I'm here. I miss my old friends and stealing drinks from rich shmucks desperate for attention. I miss short skirts and sweat-stained bras from dancing. But I am not really *that* person anymore. I have a new skin . . . stretch-marked and scratched, thanks to Archer's unclipped nails. The problem is, I haven't really figured out how to have fun in my new world. I am desperate for a social life that doesn't require flying out of state for a weekend.

Dance clubs I can get into. Mom's clubs? I don't even know where to stand in line.

I make my way downstairs in my pajamas and leopard-print coat. I take the last of my weekend cash and hit the poker table, gambling my last twenty bucks on a hand one suit short of a royal flush. Ace of hearts. King of hearts. Queen of hearts. Jack of hearts. Ten of diamonds.

I'm only a card away from having it all.

So close.

I return to my room and fall asleep just as the morning sun scrapes the horizon.

Life, if you're lucky, is only one suit short of a million-dollar hand.

"I need to make friends," I say to Frank over brunch at his place. Archer is in my lap, and the three of us nibble veggie sausage on the carpet of his Hollywood Hills apartment, thumbing through *US Weekly,* gasping at the "who wore it better" portion of the magazine.

"You have friends!" he says. "You have me!"

"I know I have you, but I think I need to make mom friends. I need to get to know some local people with kids."

"Oh. You need *mommyfriends.* I see how it is."

"It's not as easy as it sounds. It's not as organic as meeting someone at a party or moving in next door to someone and becoming best friends."

"Like us?"

"Like us. If all moms were gay men, I wouldn't have as much of a problem."

"If all moms were gay men, I think we would have bigger problems."

I know there are probably thousands of like-minded moms out there, but where do I go to find them? It isn't like dating. You can't just meet some hot piece of mama bff at the local bar. You can't just slip a phone number and pull the ole over-the-shoulder hair toss and *wink wink, nudge nudge.* I'm a fantastic flirt but a god-awful girlfriend-maker. I suck at making friends with women. I'm awkward and shy and say all the wrong things. I'm perpetually the new girl who no one invites to the slumber party.

"Maybe you should place an ad! Young Mother Seeks Vegetarian Moms with Expensive Taste."

"Who the hell would call for *her?* I sound like every other Los Angeles parent."

"Exactly," he says. "Easy, breezy."

The clouds recede as we enter the park, and Archer immediately hides between my legs and covers his ears at the first sight of playing children. After several moments in a ball at my feet, Archer untangles himself from my shoelace and takes my hand. We walk together toward the jungle gym, and every few seconds he looks back over his shoulder to make sure we aren't being followed. We wander through the playground and find a spot on the perimeter where the fence separates grassy hills from paved streets. Away from the other children. And other parents. Until we are alone.

Every time we take a trip to the park in an effort to socialize, we end up failing each other. Some children don't fit in. I didn't. Some parents don't fit in, either. I don't.

From our shady place behind a tree, we sit and watch events unfold from a distance. Archer babbles and I babble back. I feel invisible. In a good way. In a bad way. Invisible. I look out at the mothers, folded neatly beside each other on wooden benches, as their children throw sand and climb monkey bars. Archer watches them run around him in circles, and he pulls his fingers from mine and puts his hands over his eyes. He is hiding. I understand.

> ⚡ ≈.

The other day, when Archer and I crashed a Mommy & Me holiday party at the gym, I had a panic attack. I couldn't breathe with all those high-pitched voices singing ROWROWROOOOW-YOURBOAT with glazed eyes and French manicures, their children bumping into one another, all dressed in the same Gap Kids hoodies. In the sameeverythingsamesamesame.

I started to shake, and pretty soon I couldn't breathe. Archer turned around in my lap to face me. His eyes went wide before jumping out of my lap and running to the glass window, banging and scratching and flapping his arms like a caged bird.

We left immediately, hurdling over crossed legs and hand puppets on our way out the door.

I get anxiety attacks when I feel claustrophobic. In a stalled subway or an old elevator. In a controlling relationship, or an argument I cannot win. In a depression I cannot escape. And in that room at the gym, surrounded by homemade Christmas cookies and mommies and daddies and nannies and songs about spiders down the spout, I felt lost. And alone. And trapped. Like I was going to have a heart attack and die and everyone would know that my final moment in life was sitting in a stupid room singing that stupid fucking song about the spider whose livelihood depended on being washed down the drain, drying off, and climbing back up the spout. And for what? Why? *Doesn't he know? Down comes the rain to wash the spider out! It doesn't change. It's always the same story. Why does he keep coming back for more?*

I don't want to end up like that. Like the spider. Or the Gap sweatshirt with its zillions of Gap sweatshirt brothers and sisters. Because it's scary. How suddenly everyone shares a brain. Becomes the same.

Repeat after me! And no one even knows what he or she is singing. Voices blend and overlap and "Did you say that or was it me?"

I want to sing my own song.

Sometimes when I look at something or someone, all I can see is what surrounds them. All I can see is the grass and the sand and the playground. Their faces have blurred and blended, and I can't focus on their features. My depth of field is off. Maybe Archer's is too. Maybe he inherited my inability to sit neatly on a bench or play quietly with the other boys and girls. Maybe he just wants to watch. And think. Maybe he doesn't want to talk to anyone. Maybe he speaks his own language because he enjoys being in his own world, and maybe I'm more comfortable in mine.

"Earth to Rebecca. Come in, Rebecca."

"Earth to Archer. Archer? *Archhheeeer?*"

"It might be hard for a boy like that to make friends," people tell me.

It might be hard for a girl like me to make friends, too. *Real* friends. The kind with flesh and blood and hair who don't disappear or get lost. The kind you have in broad daylight, in flip-flops and jeans and no makeup.

If Archer would rather play in the corner and talk to the wall, I cannot blame him, or turn him toward the children. I too feel more myself in the corner sometimes. And when no one's looking? I'm talking to the wall too.

Every day I look at Archer and am able to better understand myself. And I wonder if perhaps his idiosyncrasies are as much my own. His hypersensitivity to his surroundings. His apprehension. The way he hides when he is unable to respond. Sometimes when I look at Archer, I see my own lost truths, bold as the stripes in his eyes.

I give myself an F for effort. We've been at the park for almost two hours, and I have yet to say a word to anyone. A couple of head nods are all. A smile. The clouds disappear to make room for the sun, and Archer grabs for my sunglasses to put them over his eyes.

"Are you ready to go?"

The clouds return as we pull out of the parking lot, and after several moments of adjusting the rearview mirror, I refocus and start to recognize myself again. But just in case, I look back over my shoulder to make sure we aren't being followed.

We drive through the back streets toward home, where iron

gates separate unmanaged yards from managed ones. Away from the other children and parents until we are alone.

"How did it go? Did you meet anyone nice?" Frank asks over the phone.

"Not really," I answer. "I suck."

"Aw. You will," he reassures.

I'm too ashamed to admit to him that I didn't even try.

"I hope so," I say.

And I really want to mean it.

MAKE
New Friends

"CAPTAIN ARCHER, Pirate of the Snails!" I yell, chasing after Archer with a hanger for a hook in my sleeve.

He giggles insanely and runs full speed into the wall, where he bumps his face and falls with a thud backward into my arms. I remove my eye patch and scream before Archer has time to react. Blood spews out of his face like a geyser.

"Oh my god! Oh my god! Oh my god!" I'm running around in circles trying to think, think, *think!*

I grab a wad of toilet paper and press it over his eyebrow. Archer pushes my hand away and starts to cry. Children are funny. They don't cry when they hit their heads. They only cry when you try to make it better. Getting hurt is the greatest way to get attention. This is a problem for people big and small, I think. We receive the most love when we hurt ourselves.

As soon as I stop howling, Archer does too.

Funny how that works.

The last time I saw Archer's blood was when I accidentally cut the top of his finger off with the fingernail clippers. I haven't cut his nails since. I just let them grow until they break off, which they eventually do, but not before they become freakish human talons. There is no way to avoid drawing blood from a kid who thrashes any time I come near him with nail clippers, even in his sleep. I can't really blame him though.

The blood is soaking through the toilet paper, but Archer doesn't seem to mind. He has suddenly become fixated on the palm trees out the window.

"Maybe no more pirate games," I sigh.

He looks at me with the face of a warrior and pushes himself backward off the couch and onto his feet, running once again full speed ahead to the nearest wall. Except this time at the very last second he leans to the left, to safety.

He's learning, I think, and I chase after him toward his bedroom.

"I'm going to get you, Bloody Toilet Paper Face!"

Our days mainly consist of chasing each other in circles until one of us gets hurt. Sometimes, when we're both tired and neither of us feels like napping, we eat Cheerios straight from the box and watch *Sesame Street* side by side.

We take hour-long nature walks around the block, pausing at every crack in the sidewalk so Archer can take a moment to smell every flower. Every leaf. He hugs the trees and jumps in the damp spots on the pavement, even though there isn't water enough to splash. I make up our own songs, and invite Archer to join me if ever he decides to sing along.

As a child, I could never decipher the words to the songs I heard. It was easier to make them up. "Too many walls have been built in between us" became "Too many balls have been nailed to my penis," and strangely I never questioned the oddities of such lyrics.

Archer reaches for the water bottle in the back of his stroller. It has been leaking for the past block and a half; a trail of water spots leads from home to the place we are standing.

"Twinkle twinkle little Arch,
How I wonder, are you parched?

Archer grunts and gulps the water, smiling.

Smelling flowers on our walk.
Will you ever learn to talk?
Twinkle twinkle little Arch,
How I wonder, are you parched?"

He hands the bottle back to me, and I stop singing. Helicopters swarm overhead like angry birds, and Archer swoons, tripping and falling on his face in the process. He looks up at me, waiting for me to gasp, but I don't.

"You're okay," I say, watching as a goose egg appears seconds later.

His frown fades, and off he goes again like nothing happened.

I'm learning too.

I get self-conscious when Archer has a scar or a bruise or a scratch on his face.

"What happened to him?" people ask, waiting, it feels like, for me to make excuses.

"He fell and hit his face on the wall," I tell them, but by the looks on their faces I might as well have muttered, "Oh, that? He just walked into my fist. No big deal."

I'll admit that before I had Archer, I would be suspicious of little children with black eyes and bruises on their faces. I hadn't thought that toddlers—being new at the whole walking, running, stair-climbing thing—quite regularly took spills.

Now I understandably collect dirty looks as my karma for flashing those same looks before I knew better.

I'm trying to maintain a happy balance of "playmate" and "disciplinarian" for Archer, so I feel conflicted when I come home to Archer and Hal sliding around a flooded kitchen on their bellies in their underwear, laughing and shivering. I'm usually the first to let Archer splash in puddles, even with his new shoes on, but water fights in the house? That's a bit much. I want to join them, but I don't. *I shouldn't,* so I stare at them and wait for them to read my mind.

But they don't.

"Where on earth did all this water come from?" I finally ask, with all the authority I have in me. I cross my arms over my chest and twist my face into a scowl.

"The dog bowl. Archer was splashing in it, and then it spilled."

"So . . . you decided to swim in it?"

"Why not?"

"Why not? Why not? *Why not?*" (Note: always repeat questions three times for effect. Very bosslike. Very powerful sounding.) "It's fifty degrees in here, that's why not! And the dog water is a bacteria asylum! And Archer has a cold." *Oh my god . . . did I just say that?*

"Anything else?"

I think for a moment. "No. That's all. Those are my reasons."

"Okay," Hal says, turning to Archer. "Let's go get dressed."

I'm proud of my authoritativeness but also wildly jealous that at this moment Hal gets to be the playmate, which apparently makes me the police. *I* want to be the fun one. *Can't I be the fun one?*

I think the main reason I wanted a boy so badly is because I wanted to live vicariously through one. I was jealous of boys as a child. They had pet snakes and weren't afraid of spiders. I wanted to become one of them, to skateboard without being pushed away.

"Leave us alone," they would tell me.

"Just pretend I'm a boy like you," I begged. But no one ever could. I was a *girl,* and I resented that.

I have been looking forward to revisiting my childhood wish by doing boyish things with Archer—exploring the deep seas of our imaginations with guns ablazin' and packs of wild dogs, building skateboard ramps out of plywood and fishing poles out of popsicle sticks, wondering if it would be possible to defy the mother-son relationship, to challenge Archer to a duel with an empty roll of wrapping paper, my sword.

Hal plays with Archer differently from the way I do. Playing in water on the kitchen floor is not the same as dressing up like pirates. Maybe that's why Archer runs to Hal when he wants to play, his hands full of objects to toss or read or tear apart. Maybe he knows I'm not a boy. I smell different. I like to get my hands dirty, just not dirty enough.

I watch Hal strip Archer down to his diaper. He fumbles through Archer's carefully folded clothes and picks out a shirt and a pair of pants that don't match. I open my mouth to say something but catch myself. I don't want it to matter to me but it does.

Just leave Hal alone.

But that shirt looks ridiculous with those pants! I can't stand here any longer and say nothing.

I come out of hiding and make a beeline to Archer's dresser. I unfold several T-shirts before I find one to match his green cords.

"Here. This shirt matches," I proclaim, interfering.

Hal and Archer look at me like I'm crazy. Like I'm an alien weirdo freak. A mom.

I'm a mom.

"I'm sorry," I say guiltily. "You can put him in whatever you want."

I hope this doesn't mean we can't catch crawdads and build forts. I still really want to build forts.

I'm at the Dragonfly Dulou, a boutique–slash–meeting place for various mom groups and birthday parties. It's my first time. I'm here to meet a new friend.

Charlotte and I found each other in perfect postmodern fashion: on the Internet. We exchanged a few emails and decided last Monday to meet here, today, at the boutique where I am waiting. I'm trying to stay calm, but I'm so goddamn nervous I'm sweating. The only thing worse than a blind date is a blind date with a woman who also happens to be a mother with a son Archer's age. I don't want to blow this. *Please don't blow this.*

The Dragonfly Dulou is buzzing with attractive moms

accessorized with the latest mommy gadgets, prepared with every kind of health snack imaginable. *I am not this together*, I think, but I take out my baggie of Cheerios and place it on the mat so I seem like I am.

"These? They're organic," I say, in case anybody's listening.

Other than that, I don't say much. I adjust Archer, who is cemented to my lap with a glorious concoction of sweat and drool, and count the stains in the cement.

The class begins, and Charlotte still isn't here.

Christ, she's totally standing me up! She hates me. She saw me through the window and hated my hair. I slept on it weird and my bangs are all sticking up and I look really boring. I should have put more thought into this outfit. I shouldn't have worn camo, but I wanted to blend in.

Maybe she died! That would be just my luck. My first potential mom friend and POW, hit by a bus on her way to meet me.

"Hey, Charlotte," one of the other moms calls out, and I turn my head, like in slow motion. She walks in, waving to the other mothers with her baby in her arms. Her hair is long and dark, and she's wearing the same Converse Chuck Taylors without the shoelaces that I have on, except hers look brand-new.

Archer smashes his face between my boobs, and I smile.

"Rebecca?" she asks.

"I am. And you, I presume, must be Charlotte."

I did not just say "presume," did I? Yikes. I sound like a Young

Republican. Next I'll try to shake her hand with a soggy palm and offer to show her my gun collection.

"This is Archer. He's shy."

"This is Jackson," she says, pointing to her little boy, whose head is also smashed against her chest. He has a black eye to complement Archer's scabbed-over gash. "He's shy too."

She sits down beside me, and I plead with Archer to come out from hiding. He slowly turns himself around, his snot attached to my shirt like a spider web. Jackson gets up and wobbles off on his feet. It takes some time, but eventually Archer does too.

They don't play together, but they wander around in their own little worlds, side by side, falling and getting back up.

"Jackson just started walking."

"Archer too!"

Coincidences abound. We're both writers. Our husbands are both musicians. We both broke a nail earlier in the afternoon. It's petty for me to be so concerned with these things but it's too late. I'm trapped inside a romantic comedy, watching as our future flashes before me in montage form, complete with soundtrack and freeze-frames:

* Laughing on the swing set with our boys in our laps after meeting for coffee
* Pushing our strollers along the winding paths of the zoo
* Drawing elephants on the sidewalk with pink chalk

* Exchanging books and music and make-up tips
* Telling secrets

The music swells in my imaginary music video, and pretty soon we're dancing around in circles, singing "Ring around the Rosy" in high-contrast light, like an early '90s music video.

I manage to sit through the entire class without listening to a single word. I nod and smile and pick Archer's boogers and think about how glad I am that Charlotte didn't get run over by a bus.

"Hey. They just opened a Pinkberry on Santa Monica. We could hit up the West Hollywood Park and grab yogurt afterward," she suggests.

"I'd love to," I say, wrangling Archer, who's upset that I won't let him eat a dead bee.

"How about Monday?"

I have plans Monday, but I don't care. "That sounds perfect," I say.

And I mean it. I can't wait.

BABY,
It's Cool Outside

✳

CHARLOTTE AND I eat ice cream side by side as Archer and Jackson waddle toward the swing set. I have never been to this park before, but it seems to be popular. Maybe because the trendy yogurt place is so close. Or maybe it's just cool here.

All of the other moms seem to know one another. They give each other high-fives and talk loud enough so that everyone can hear them. I am usually a spy, eavesdropping on other people's conversations, stealing strangers' whispers, paraphrasing in my moleskin, but today I don't have to spy. There is nothing quiet about their conversations.

"My son Dax is like soooooo cute in his brand-new rugby polo!"

"Totally hot. Did you get it at Babystyle? I have the *same* one for Max!"

"Don't look now. Carrie's little boy is driving a kid-size Hummer H2. What was she thinking?"

"Doesn't she know about the hybrid tricycle? Ryder and Storm each have one."

"So, like, my pediatrician said that his pediatrician said that his pediatrician said . . . "

"No way. My pediatrician's dog's veterinarian's friend's pediatrician's mom said that was totally not true."

"Well *I* read that if you breastfeed your children until kindergarten they will be better listeners."

"Well *I* read that if you breastfeed your husband, he'll be a better listener."

"Seriouslynoway. Did you read that in Spock or Sears?"

"Ohmigawd! Don't look now. DILF alert!"

"He is *not* pushing the Rock Star stroller. Such a Bugaboo knockoff. Gay men should know better."

"I can't believe his daughter, Waterfall, didn't get into the Webster Private School for infants."

"It's *such* a great school."

"So, ladies, *gather* round. I just got my photos back from Annie Leibovitz! She took photos of Neruda, did I not tell you?"

"So not fair."

"Well, I have booked Wolfgang Puck to cater Siren's six-month birthday bash."

"Well I bought Rain backstage passes to see the Wiggles Friday night!"

The women gasp. Rain's mother has won. She has the most impressive news of all.

"Oh my *god*. The Wiggles? The Wiggles!"

I don't know who the hell "the Wiggles" are, but apparently they're big-time. I didn't realize such bands existed for toddlers. I just figured Raffi still had the market cornered, all these years later.

I gotta shake, shake, shake my sillies out and wiggle my waggles away.

"Have you ever heard of the Wiggles?" I ask Charlotte.

"Of course!"

Shit.

"Yeah. Me too," I lie. "They're great. We have all their records. B-sides, bootlegs. Imports . . . "

"No way! The Wiggles have bootlegs?"

I swallow. "Mmm-hmm. Tons," I continue to fib, trying to sound cool and exclusive.

Apparently, I'm from outer space. The Wiggles are an international sensation, along with a dude named Dan Zanes (who looks like Drop Dead Fred) and about a thousand other toddler-rock, indie darlings for children—not a single one of which I have heard of.

"I've never heard of them either, so don't feel bad," Hal assures. "Who knew there was a whole world of kids' music?"

But I should know, I think. It used to be my life . . . to know.

It's a Saturday night and I'm making plans to go out for drinks with my cousin, Erica, who is visiting from out of town.

"Let's go somewhere cool, Bec."

"Okay!"

I think for a moment. *Cool. Where is cool?* "How about . . . uhh, heh, um."

I have no idea where to take her. The turnaround for cool hipster joints is pretty quick, and I'm, hmmm, let's see . . . about two years behind. *No. Really? Has it been that long?*

"Honestly, Erica? I don't have a clue what's cool anymore."

She shrugs. "That's fine. We can go somewhere uncool. I don't really care."

But I do. I used to know these things, and now I don't. Seven years in Los Angeles and I know about as much of my city's nightlife as an out-of-towner with a Zagat guide.

God, I'm such a mom.

"I'll call Frank," I suggest. "He'll know where to send us."

Not so long ago, Frank would have been the one to call *me*. In those days I knew the back doors to the right bars, how to crash Oscar parties and get into sold-out shows. My hair was either black or red or platinum blonde—short and styled into some kind of asymmetrical high-maintenance bob that needed an hour of primping every morning—and my wardrobe consisted of band tees and jeans, big earrings and heavy eye makeup. I was spirited and spontaneous, throwing down what cash I had on me for a new tattoo at a dirty parlor, making memories out of experiences as I grabbed life with both fists.

My nights were spent at live-music venues and dive bars, tipping back vodka tonics and shooting pool, occasionally devoting weekends to road trips up north to Bay Area venues and secret shows. The sounds from my stereo, always loud, masked my loneliness. I scribbled down lyrics with mechanical pencils, trapping erasable answers to questions I didn't know I had. I collected band T-shirts and kept all of my ticket stubs in my underwear drawer. Obscure bands were my specialty, and I studied them with the same kind of determination that friends crammed for exams, listening to college radio at all hours of the night, downloading tracks, and digging through piles of rare finds at local record stores and garage sales. I made hundreds of mix tapes and passed them out to friends and people I'd met only once. "These are the hottest new bands," I would say. The *coolest* new bands.

I considered myself a self-made music aficionado to such a degree that while living in Europe, the summer I was nineteen, I persuaded a magazine to send me on location to international music festivals, working as a journalist with no journalistic experience. Passionate and fearless, I booked meetings with a blank portfolio and the kind of confidence that could only come from teenage naivete, even though I had lied and said I was twenty-five. I made friends with local bands and went on tour with the sweaty rockers I met while traveling, once tagging along in the back of a tour van for eight hours with an amp between my legs and plug-ins tangled at my ankles. And as I watched the back roads of the English countryside unravel like yarn through the stagnant smoke of spliffs, I never once worried how I would find my way home. I just studied the world through the cracked back windows, always along for the ride.

I have forgotten how that feels, that particular brand of freedom, the things you take for granted before you become a parent. When responsibility is just an option and there is all the time in the world for keeping up with the coolest bars and newest bands and road tripping with strangers to dead ends.

In my previous life, my evening ritual before a night on the town consisted of a ten-outfit costume change. Now I grab the first clean shirt and jeans I can find. My once-organized shoes are now tossed about. I duck beneath clothes racks in search of a decent pair, on my hands and knees, until I find a match. I scrape dried string-cheese off the insole and slip them on. The earrings that used to skim my shoulders are tangled in their box from neglect. It's too risky wearing them now. I'll have to wait until Archer is old enough to listen when I tell him not to pull them out of my ears.

Tonight, I opt for bangles. Bangles are the only accessory both child-friendly and chic. I shake my wrists so they jingle, like old times. Some things have to change. But not everything. Some things can stay the same.

We seat ourselves outside on the patio for better people-watching. The outsiders are always more interesting than the those on the inside, who sulk in the shadows with their bottles and private parties.

"Frank recommended this place," I tell Erica. "I've never heard of it."

"It's nice. I like it!"

"Me too."

This is fun, I think. I need to get out more often. I miss the darkness and the smell of vodka and being with people my age. I miss my cousin and smoke in the air and the bums that puke in the alleys behind lantern-trimmed hot spots.

And then I hear my name being called from the street.

"Becca? Is that you?"

I turn around to see an old friend walking toward our table in kitten heels and layers of plastic accessories. Her makeup is flawless: dark smoky eyes, red lipstick. Her jeans are perfectly tapered. I am immediately self-conscious about my outfit. It was cold so I brought a pashmina. *A fucking pashmina.* A fine choice for the Westside, but not for Hollywood. Hollywood is plastic accessories and layered baby-doll dresses and skinny jeans under wide belts with gold buckles. My jeans are boot-cut. I might as well have tattooed MOM on my forehead.

"Hey Kel!"

"It's been *forever!*"

"I know it!"

"How's the baby?"

"He's good. And you?"

"Good! Very good! This is my boyfriend, Patrick. We're just about to go see the Elected at the El Rey."

"The what?"

"You know . . . the Elected?"

I shake my head. "I've never heard of them."

Her eyes go wide before shrugging. Her boyfriend flashes me the "I'm better than you" eyes, and I curl at the edges like an old photograph.

I shake my wrists so she takes notice of my bangles. *My bangles.*

"I haven't really kept up with the music scene. I'm super busy and . . . "

"Well, they're really good. You should check them out. You know, if you have time or whatever."

"Yeah. Okay. Have a fun show."

Kelly and her boyfriend turn and walk off, their matching tattoos exposed through her backless tunic and his mangled band tee. I unwrap my pashmina from my shoulders and take a swig of my cocktail, feeling like a sore thumb amid the ashes of Parliament Lights and Pabst Blue Ribbon.

I am a tourist in my own town. I'm on the outside. And even if I could back into a corner with my cigarettes and sunglasses, it would be too dark, too late, too different.

"I shouldn't have worn a pashmina, I hate pashminas," I say, even though it isn't true. I just don't want to look like the type who wears one. My mom wears a pashmina. I draw stereotypes to protect myself but isolate myself instead.

"I think it's pretty," Erica assures. "It looks good on you."

I don't know if "cool" has a lifespan. I think maybe it just changes. The indie kids sell out or settle down or don't have time for their old lives, but I don't want to end up alone without my soundtrack.

I make a promise to myself to stay until last call, but by 10:00 PM I'm yawning. Erica smiles and says, "It's okay. We can go home. I'm tired too."

I shake my head. "I'm not tired." I smack myself repeatedly in the face. "See? I could go out all night. In fact, maybe we should go try to catch that band?"

I may have grown out my hair and outgrown my party-girl days, but I can still rock out. Growing up doesn't mean growing out of my favorite shoes—not if they make me happy, not if they're good for dancing. Just like becoming a parent doesn't mean laser tattoo removal and moving to the suburbs. I can have it all. I don't have to say goodbye to everything.

Some things don't have to change.

We leave the bar and the warmth of its outdoor heating lamps and follow the pavement to our parking meter. I untie my pashmina from my hobo bag and fling it over my shoulders. It's freezing out here, and I'd rather be warm than cool.

I sit down beside Archer, who is leaning over the pavement, watching the ants.

"Ooooooh," he says, babbling on to them as they march by.

"The ants go marching one by one, hoorah, hoorah!" I sing as loud as I can, and Archer claps and jumps up and down, humming along as loud as he can like an amplifier, reaching toward my wrist with concentration. He traces over my tattoos with his fingers, pressing the stars on my wrists like they are buttons. He scratches at them, trying to pick them off my skin. But of course, he can't. No one can.

Archer keeps pressing on my wrist, scratching, twisting, reading, so I trace the same lines with him, and I tell him the story of where each mark has come from, the beautiful scars.

"You can try to scratch them away," I say, "but these words will never change." *Just like my love for you.*

Archer is a permanent mark on me, much like the ivy on my foot or the flower petals that fall down my hip, a lifetime commitment and souvenir of moments lived without doubt or hesitation—a personal pact made with the future to never let go of the past.

I may not have the hair or the wardrobe or know where the backdoor bars are anymore, but that's okay. I have Archer: my ultimate rebellion. *Having a baby is like getting a tattoo on your soul.*

I will never forget where I have been, and I have Archer to remind me where I'm going, drifting, perhaps farther and farther from "the scene" that once defined me. And that's okay. I can be on the outside. I'm getting pretty comfortable chilling on my stoop with my favorite dude, rocking out to songs about ants marching and stars twinkling and baby beluga in the deep blue sea. There is no place I would rather be than here, even if "cool" has taken on a new, more literal meaning.

Archer shivers as I pull his arms through the sleeves of his sweater.

SILHOUETTES

MY MOTHER AND I are at war—the kind of war where exple-
tives and the occasional object are hurled, and my mother sobs and
I throw my hands up and shake my head and say, "You're not listening to me!" And then my mother scolds me for treating her like
shit. The kind of war we used to wage against one another when I
was fifteen. And sixteen. And seventeen . . . until I moved out of my
parents' house to Los Angeles, to live on my own. We stopped fighting after that. Maybe I grew out of it, or maybe it was the distance
between us that made the time we spent together precious, non-
confrontational. We squabbled, but it was never like this.

I slam the door.

"Fucking bitch!" I scream into my hands. We're yelling at one
another from both sides of my old bedroom door.

Everything looks the same in here, my old pictures of friends
and the dried roses from ex-boyfriends hanging in the window,

knotted with twine, the skateboard stickers peeling on my mir-rored closet doors: Zero and Planet Earth and Independent Truck Company.

My mother and I speak on the phone every day, sometimes even on the hour. We have the same dreams sometimes and finish one another's sentences. We're best friends. And even as a teenager with a sharp tongue and wild eyes, I knew there was no woman in the world I would rather call "Mom."

"Open this door!"

"Go away! Leave me alone!"

"Jesus, Rebecca!"

"Jesus, *Mom.*"

"You misunderstood me!"

"No I didn't. I know exactly what you meant. *Exactly.*"

She scurries down the hall crying, and I let go of the doorknob and fall on my knees at the foot of my bed. *I wish she would come back. I don't want her to cry. I don't want to be alone right now.*

Like most fights, it started over a simple miscommunication. Apparently, while I was away on a business/pleasure vacation in Austin, Archer slept through the night. He also ate everything put in front of him and was happy and perfect and wonderful and "the most pleasurable human being to be around."

His perfect behavior ended the second I came home, when immediately he turned to tantrums and refused to sleep or eat any-thing other than Cheerios.

"While you were gone, I gave him one hundred percent of my attention," my mom had said. "Maybe that's why he was so good."

I took this to mean that because I was unable to give Archer one hundred percent of my attention I was a shitty mother, and therefore, my child hated me and refused to sleep or eat or be happy—that he would grow up to curse the day he had ever been born because I was unable to be the kind of mother my mom was for me, the kind who dropped everything for her children. The kind of mother who would never even *think* to take a five-day working vacation away from her family, getting drunk on free booze and rocking out to bands and flirting with strangers in dark, overcrowded bars. The kind of mother who didn't mind clipped wings, who didn't have to work shit out or rebel against her own life.

I remember only one fight between my parents during my childhood. I thought for sure they would be getting a divorce because I was so shocked to hear them yell at one another. *It isn't normal. This must be the end of their marriage.* Most of my friends' parents were divorced at the time, so it seemed highly likely that eventually mine would be too. I called my friend crying.

"I think my parents are going to get a divorce," I said. My friend had been dealing with her parents' divorce, and I wanted her to know I might soon be in the same boat.

"Why? What happened?"

"They're fighting right now."

"Yeah . . . ?"

"I've never heard them fight before."

"Becca, sometimes parents fight."

"Oh."

I was old enough to know better, but how could I? My parents managed to keep their marital problems to themselves. I never once doubted my parents' perfection. Even as a teenager, when I wanted so desperately to be damaged. I craved heartbreak and tragedy and went looking for sadness, if only to break free from the sunshine. *Why can't it just rain on me!* I wanted to feel challenged, emotionally shipwrecked, but how could I under a roof where there was always so much love?

"You're lucky," my friends told me.

And I was, but at the time I just wanted to be fucked-up like everyone else. I needed to push the boundaries to find out what it felt like to fall and break. So I threw myself at boys I knew would hurt me and girls who could teach me the ropes of rebellion until I could stand on my own platform, wounded, without fear.

I was embarrassed by my family. I was ashamed of our closeness—the duets my brother and mother strummed on their guitars as my sister played her flute in the next room and my dad belted out the wrong words to the familiar songs. We were the town Partridge Family, a flock of creative fools in matching smocks holding hands. And I wanted no part of it.

"I'm sorry that I can't be the mother you are! I'm sorry I am totally fucked-up and selfish and want to be alone once in a while! I'm sorry that I will never be *you!* I really am."

"I never said that! I think you are an amazing mother! You're a better mother than I am in so many ways!" my mother cries. But she's lying. She *has to* be lying.

And even if she isn't I need to believe right now that she is. I need to think for a second that she's against me, because I feel alone, and her being here for me changes that. *Just give me a second. Let me feel like I have no one. Give me a moment of emptiness. Why do you have to be there for me all the time? Go away, please. Just for a moment, and then you can come back.*

"Well you're a fucking perfect mother and I'm just . . . I didn't want to come home. I *don't* want to go home. What kind of mother doesn't want to come home to her family?"

And suddenly I'm a little girl again, in my mother's arms, and all of my questions and worries and fears stream down my face and through the cracks of my broken facade, the secrets I have kept from her and the anger I have been unable to express. And *whooooosh*—I have flooded us both with words I can't make sense of, washing us away like Alice in Wonderland in the tears that almost drowned her.

My mother raises her hand. "I'm that kind of mother," she says. "There were plenty of times when I didn't want to come home either. That's just part of having a family and being in a marriage and living a life."

"Really?"

"It wasn't all sunshine for me when you kids were growing

up, just so you know. I struggled. I got lost. I may have hidden most of it from you, but I know how you feel. I'm sure every mother does."

And suddenly she is human. My mom is imperfect. She has secrets too. And when I look at her I see myself and every woman and mother and wife, all of us torn between two worlds, tempted to pull away from time to time. *We all feel that way sometimes.*

I used to read my journal to my mom late at night, bad poetry and short stories that I wished were nonfiction, sometimes until the sun came up. Or sometimes we would just lie next to one another, eyes swollen shut from crying, voices hoarse from screaming, holding hands and humming along to the stereo.

"It's a school night," my mom would say. "You need to get up early." Except she would stay with me. She wouldn't leave until I was tired, until I had exhausted my stories and had nothing but silence to say.

"Archer will be up soon," she warns. "You really need your sleep."

"But wait!" I say, "I almost forgot to tell you. . . . "

And she stays, without once checking her watch, even though I know she's tired, her eyes red and swollen from the tears I caused. I tell her about how scary the flight home was, how we got stuck in a thunderstorm and how the guy who was sitting next to me was squeezing my hand really hard because he was terrified. "Everything is going to be okay," I said, even though I thought we were all going to die.

"All I could think about was Archer and all the things I would miss and whether or not he would remember me. And Hal and I had fought the night before and I was so sorry because I really do love him even though we have our moments of craziness. And then I remembered what you said to me when I first learned to drive. You told me to visualize a force field around the car, so that's what I did. I closed my eyes and imagined a giant rainbow around the airplane and I squeezed the stranger's hand and I said, *I'm so lucky, I'm so lucky, I'm so lucky* over and over until the passengers stopped yelping and the man beside me stopped crying and the flight attendants' voices weren't shaky anymore and I knew we had escaped the storm. I've never been afraid to fly before, but suddenly I was all alone, my head in the clouds as free as I could be, praying for the turbulence to stop, for steadiness."

"You wanted to be home?"

"I did."

I look up to the glow-in-the-dark stars still stuck to my ceiling all these years later and I wonder why my mom hasn't taken them down, if she's waiting for me to. My room is exactly as I left it when I moved out. Maybe in a way she doesn't want to let go. Maybe neither of us do.

"I used to write the names of all the boys I wanted to kiss on those stars," I tell her. "And then I would wish on them."

"Did they ever come true?" she asks.

"Some of them," I say.

"Not all wishes are supposed to, you know. Only the good ones."

"Thank you for watching Archer while I was gone."

"Thank you for coming home."

And we hold hands, two silhouettes in the window I used to climb out of in the middle of the night, plotting my escape into the adult world.

I always assumed I would outgrow my need for my mother, but I haven't. Our relationship has changed through the years, evolved, but I still need her just as much as I always did, maybe even more than ever.

Sometimes mothers need their mothers too.

ALL IS
Full of Love

ARCHER IS ONE AND three-quarters old today, and although three-quarters might not seem as significant as turning one, or even two, it is to me. It doesn't feel like so long ago that I introduced myself in halves and three-quarters and thirds.

"How old are you?"

"I'm ten and a half. How old are you?"

"Eight and three-quarters."

As children we understood perfectly. And as a parent, I do again.

"How old is your child?"

"Sixteen weeks," or "Seventeen months," or "Forty-seven months," which is usually when I have to do the math on my fingers. Before I had a child, it annoyed me when a mother rattled off her children's ages in months, like I was supposed to know the difference between thirteen months and twenty-six months and thirty-three months. I figured it was just some strange parent language, and apparently it is, because now that I have a child, I get it.

When you have a baby, every day counts. Every week matters. Every month is a revelation, a collection of milestones so vast it's easy to forget that they have even happened.

"Take my finger," I say, holding my pointer finger for Archer to grab as he walks down the stairs, but instead he grabs for my whole hand. Our palms are against each other, and our fingers meet at the tips, and we continue down the stairs for the very first time, hand in hand.

The first time I held Archer, seconds after he was born, he took hold of my pinky and squeezed so tight it almost hurt. And I remember thinking, *How strong you are, little baby.* I was so overcome by the tightness of his grasp, the miracle of a human so small, now out in the world, squeezing with all of his might.

"It's a reflex," they told me. "Hold your pinky out, and he will grab on. He won't let go." He didn't and I was glad.

Not long after, he grabbed for my other fingers too—my ring finger and my pointer finger and my thumb. And when he was learning to walk, he would hold two fingers, one from each hand, and I'd say, "Come on! You can do it!" and he'd smile and fall on his face, his hands slipping from my fingers, until he grabbed on again to pull himself back up. *Hold on tight!*

Now his hand is too big for just a finger. He is too big for fingers. Yesterday he wasn't, but today he is. *Just like that.*

I often try to place my finger in Archer's hand, waiting for it to wrap around me like an anemone. But it doesn't. The finger reflex is gone. Just like the startling reflex, when babies raise their hands and shake their arms if they're sleeping and someone makes a loud sound.

I squeeze Archer's hand in mine, and he looks back at me and smiles, pulling me down the street. *Follow me, Mommy. Let's go this way.* And I follow him, holding on tight, trying as best I can not to mourn the days when my finger was so big Archer had no choice but to hold on and not let go.

"Okay, dude. *Sesame Street*'s all done!"

Archer protests, flailing his arms like failing wings.

"Nope. You can see Elmo tomorrow though."

"Eh," he says. *"Ehhhhhh."*

Archer's eyes get squinty and his lip curls. His chest heaves, and a deep groan penetrates the small space between us. I've never heard this sound before, and it catches me off guard. It's a mean noise, an extremely pissed-off *I hate you, Mom* noise, and oh my god, he's going to punch me in the . . .

"Ahahahahaha!" he chuckles like a deranged psychopath.

"What the fuck?" I say. "I mean . . . what the funk?" I don't usually swear in front of Archer, but I'm bleeding, spitting contents from my broken lip into my hands.

"Ahahahahahahaha," he laughs again, this time harder than before.

"No hitting! Are you crazy?"

Archer laughs devilishly and punches me again. I should have known to block him, but I am so shocked at his sudden violence that I am helpless to defend myself. And even though Archer's new hobbies happen to include page-ripping and dog-biting and the occasional head-butt, this is the first time I've been punched in the face.

I wipe my throbbing lip.

This sucks.

"You made Mommy bleed! Look at this stuff coming out of my face! That's owwie juice! That's what happens when you hurt somebody. Not nice. Yucky."

Archer's laughs become hysterics, and I am tempted to cage him and call an exorcist. There is a medium-size possibility I am raising a serial killer.

"You think this is funny? You think punching Mommy in the face is something to laugh about?"

Archer lunges at me, a flying leap off the couch, and kicks me in the boob with his new hard-soled shoes. I clutch my chest. Somebody needs to stop him before he kills me.

"Son of a bitch!" I say, quickly realizing I just called myself a bitch, which is even more upsetting in my current situation, bloody and dying on the floor of my house with Archer proudly looking on.

The door swings open. It's Hal.

"Oh thank god, you're home! You've got to help me! Archer's trying to kill me. . . . I'm bleeding out of my head and my left boob is broken."

Archer smiles at his daddy and gives him a giant kiss on the lips.

"Mmmmmaaaah," he says.

"He's possessed! We're raising a psychopath!"

"He's only hitting you because he loves you," Hal says. "He doesn't hit me."

"That's insane! He loves you just as much! He should be punching your face too!"

"I wish he would!" he says. "I want to be loved."

"I want to be loved too, like a normal person. Kisses and cuddles, not punches and kicks."

"Maybe he's just tired."

"Great. You can put him down for a nap. I'm too injured."

The terrible twos, it seems, have come a few months early. I was warned of this period but not advised that I would need self-defense classes in order to get through it.

"It'll pass," my mother says on the phone. "Your sister used to be the same way. I worried about her for years. He's just learning where his boundaries are. He'll be fine."

"He's crazy! I don't even like him right now! I mean, who does that? And then laughs about it?"

"Don't talk like that. Of course you like him. You love him!"

"Not right now," I say, but the minute I utter the words I immediately regret them. The truth is that Archer could beat my ass as much as he wants to and I'll still love him in insane ways. *Runaway Bunny* style: *If you go flying on a flying trapeze . . . I will be a tightrope walker and I will walk across the air to you.*

Motherhood is masochism at its finest.

If you should become frustrated, then I will become a punching bag you beat to a pulp so you feel better.

And I will always come back for more, even on days when being a parent is like trying to rescue bees from a swimming pool.

Ouch! He stung me. Ouch! He stung me again.

The swelling goes down by the time Archer wakes up from his nap, and I am almost myself again. I watch as my devil child babbles out the window at the birds as he so often does when he wakes up from a long and much-needed nap. He is almost perfect again, my sweet little boy with the saucer eyes and drool-soaked chest.

Hal's at band practice. He and a friend have started a duo and are interviewing bass players tonight, so I decide to let bygones be bygones and make a gourmet meal for the two of us.

"As long as you're nice," I warn, and Archer smiles and hugs my legs and says, "Mmmmmmmaaaaaaaa."

"Maaaaa-meeee," I correct.

But he doesn't want to say my name. He just wants me to hold him so he can watch what I'm cooking. *Fair enough,* I think.

"Just don't punch me. . . . "

The ups and downs are extreme. The highs and lows are almost blindsiding. Because of the love. So much love.

Archer takes a seat in my lap in the middle of the kitchen floor. I pull the wok of risotto off the counter, and he opens his mouth wide like a baby bird. He makes a face. The risotto is too hot, so he spits it out in his hand and gives it to me. I blow it and press it with my finger until it cools, and scoop it up on my spoon, offering it back to him. Archer smiles and accepts with the smacking sounds he makes for more. He nods his head, swallows, and opens his mouth for seconds.

> *Twinkle twinkle, little fish,*
> *Let's eat risotto without a dish,*
> *Here's my spoon, now open wide,*
> *So I can put the food inside.*

I gather as many mushrooms as I can and cool the steamy spoonfuls with my tongue, one after another, until the bowl is empty.

The kitchen is a mess. The linoleum has browned from dirty shoes and smashed food and the splatters of olive oil. Coffee grinds are everywhere, and Archer's plastic letters are scattered under the refrigerator and the oven. We should probably be eating at the table and Archer should be in his high chair and I should mop more often, but I don't care. I don't care that my bare feet are freckled with crumbs or that neither of us have washed our hands before eating or bothered with plates, and my watermelon boxer shorts have chicken broth splatters everywhere from pouring the broth in the pan too fast. I don't even care that Archer should be using a spoon right now instead of eating in my lap, his fingers entwined in my hair as I airplane the silverware to his lips.

I wipe the excess risotto off the pan with my fingers, and Archer watches me and then does the same. Our hands encircling the giant Cephalon pot in unison, two orbits, picking up bits of rice and mushroom and shoving them slovenly in our mouths.

Right here.

Now.

This is worth all the bloody lips in the history of bleeding lips: making peace over a wok full of moist rice and mushrooms.

Archer gets up suddenly and turns to me.

"Can I please have a kiss, Mr. Bumblebee?" I ask.

He opens his mouth wide and presses his wet lips to mine, laughs, and scurries off toward his bedroom, babbling incoherently.

THINGS
That Are Relative

BE STRONG, I TELL MYSELF. *Don't cry. Just go in, hold his hand, and say something funny. You're not here to say goodbye. Not yet. You will see him again after today. Like tomorrow, for instance. You will see him tomorrow.*

Archer wants to get down but I can't let go. I need him in my arms right now, to hold me together. Just like when I was little and needed my stuffed wolf, the only thing in the world that could make everything okay. I remember watching Wolfy get fitted for his gas mask before I got my tonsils out and how it made me less afraid. I was always stronger with him in my arms, even with his ear torn off and his eyeball hanging by a thread and the stuffing coming out of his paws.

Archer squirms and flails toward the hospital floor.

"No, baby. First we have to find room 207. That's where Uncle Pete is."

My uncle has suffered from bladder cancer for several years, in and out of remission, but cancer has a way of coming back. I got the call Thursday that he wasn't going to be with us much longer.

"You need to come now and say goodbye," my mother said.

My uncle is as close as I have had to another father. I grew up riding his horses and hugging his waist on the back of his Indian motorcycle, rolling my eyes when he tried to trick me into eating bacon made from a boar he shot himself.

"Never in a million years."

"Psh," he would say, "Vegetarian."

Room 201. Room 203, 205 . . .

I knock on the door and open it slowly. My mother and sister are seated against the window, and my dad is pacing as much as one can in a room so small. Archer burrows his face in my shoulder, and as we turn the corner, there is Erica, holding her father's hand. She smiles at me.

"Hey love."

We hug and I bite my lip so hard it hurts. *Don't you dare cry, Rebecca.*

Uncle Pete's eyes are closed, but I say hello anyway. Quietly. I don't want to wake him. *Maybe this will be easier,* I think, *if he's sleeping.*

"Daddy?" Erica squeezes her dad's hand. "Rebecca and Archer are here."

Uncle Pete opens his eyes and looks over at us.

"Hey Rebecca," he says. "Hey Mr. Archer."

"Hey, Uncle Pete! What's up?" I want to sound like nothing's out of the ordinary, so I make a face and bounce Archer on my hip.

Erica gets up from her seat so I can sit down. "Hold his hand," she says.

I sit down beside him with Archer in my lap and take his hand. This is the first time I have ever held my uncle's hand, and I wonder why it took me until now.

His hands don't look sick. He squeezes my hand in his, and I can't believe how warm and strong he feels. I weep, quietly. I don't want him to know I'm sad. I didn't think he would hold on so tight. *Nothing's out of the ordinary.* But it is. Life is slipping away and to hell with being strong. I'm sad. I don't want to say good-bye. Such warm, strong hands.

I sob into Archer's hair, my face mangled and melting in his wet curls. I don't let go of either of them: my uncle's hand or Archer's little body folded in my lap, his back to me so he doesn't see me cry.

Erica comforts me. She touches my leg like everything's going to be all right and I feel guilty because *I'm* supposed to be comforting *her* and I wonder how she can be so strong without something warm to hold on to.

You're not here to say goodbye, I remind myself. *Not yet. There is always tomorrow. He will still be here tomorrow.*

And then his hand twitches. He feels around at my fingers, and suddenly, pulling his other arm out from under the bed sheet, casts an imaginary fishing rod toward the end of his bed. *Cwooooooooosh.* I can almost hear the lure breaking the water, rippling toward the horizon.

"He's been fishing," Erica explains. "He's been catching a lot of fish. Right, Daddy?"

My uncle smiles, fiddling in his imaginary tackle box before taking my hand again. *My* hand, except this time I'm the one squeezing. *Don't let go of me,* I think.

We're all together at my parents' house—worn out and sad but together, laughing and hugging and twisting each other's hair. My brother has flown in from Boston, and my sister returned a few days ago from her first year at the University of Michigan. Erica's sister Yvette is here from Spain, where she lives with her family—her husband and newborn daughter, Anushka. Yvette arrives at the house breastfeeding her daughter effortlessly and manages to give us all hugs as her baby sucks away in her sling. My nana is making herself a vodka in the kitchen, and my aunt Fran is laughing.

"I just had a very funny thought!" she says.

"Give me a hug that hurts!" my grandfather groans, standing in the doorway. Grandma Betty squeals when she sees Archer and hands me a bag of Good & Plentys on her way to kiss him. She always comes equipped with two boxes: one for me and one for Hal.

"Come give GiGi a kiss!" Grandma says, raising her youthful arms to Archer as I hug my grandpa with all my might. He is the strongest man I know, a real machine, defying age with his vigorous daily ten-mile bike rides. I've been working on my "hugs that hurt" since I was a little girl and finally, twenty-five years later, have mastered them.

"Rebecca! That hug really *did* hurt! Good one!"

"Thank you!" I say, taking a curtsy.

We gather around the table, everyone talking over each other, spilling the couscous and offering one another the food we least like in favor of our favorite things.

"Here. You want my tomatoes?"

"I'll trade you for my cucumbers. I don't eat them."

Archer reaches across my plate and pushes the couscous onto my placemat.

"Dude! That's for my mouth! Or your mouth."

"*Someone's* mouth!" my dad chimes in.

Conversation is a collage of stories and bad jokes with out-of-order punch lines and the things we cannot say out loud to friends at the risk of sounding boastful. As well as plenty of matter-of-fact comments about the food.

"Is there garlic in this? I hate garlic."

"This is the best garlic chicken I have ever tasted!"

"Aha! So there *is* garlic."

"This lettuce is especially green."

"Is it from Whole Foods or the farmers market?"

"Best lettuce I've ever tasted, hands down."

The table erupts with laughter, alive with the exuberance of a theater production. Nana interviews all of us with what remains of her English accent, hanging on by tiny strands after seventy years of living in the United States. My cousins and I have always referred to her as Nana the Banana, one of the many beloved members in a cast of professional characters. My great-aunt Dot, for instance, a spirited activist who was recently featured on the cover of *Mother Earth News* in front of a felled giant redwood tree, buck naked. She also skinny-dipped with Anaïs Nin in the early '70s and corresponded with her briefly before her death. And then there's my late great-grandmother, who claimed for all her life to be the illegitimate daughter of a Transylvanian princess. Some of my favorite childhood stories center around my nana's aunt Elizabeth—like the time she walked to town pushing her pram to show off her new baby, finding much to her surprise she had left the baby at home; or how she once visited a friend, complaining of a sharp pain in her back, finding out from said friend that the pain was coming from the wooden hanger she forgot to remove from her coat when she put it on.

The tales of Nana the Banana are not notorious, nor headline news–worthy. But they have been my defining moments for me: first as a child, chasing fairies in her garden overlooking the sea; then as a teenager, traveling the world as her companion; and now as a woman, following in her career footsteps, exchanging emails, and sharing our stories and the chapters of the books we write simultaneously.

Nana leans over and whispers something in Archer's ear. She smiles, raises her eyebrows, and checks his face for recognition.

"What are you two talking about?" I ask.

"Oh, nothing. Just old times."

"Old times?"

"Yes, you know. This and that. I ran into a mutual acquaintance of ours this afternoon."

"Um. Okay."

I have no idea what she's talking about. It isn't like Nana to speak so seriously about something so absurd.

⇒ ⅳ ⇐

"Nana said she was talking to Archer about old times," I say, loading the dishwasher with my mother after the last guest has gone home.

"I know." My mother hesitates. "Nana thinks Archer is the reincarnation of Grandpa Lou. She thinks he's come back to be with the family."

My grandpa Lou, a Superior Court judge, passed away ten years ago. He died of cancer too.

"She said that to you?"

"On many occasions, actually. She had a dream he came to her and said so. I think it's sweet. It's given her a whole new lease on life."

"But Archer's her great-grandchild! She's not supposed to think he's her husband! That's insane!"

"Maybe. But what does it matter if it makes her happy?"

Erica was married this morning in her father's hospice room so he could be there to give her away. I found her a last-minute dress and new shoes, and her fiancé a shirt to match. My aunt Fran made bouquets and boutonnieres out of red and pink roses from her garden, and Nana brought the Moët and peach juice for a Bellini toast. A friend ministered the service on the patio outside the hospice room, and using his last bit of strength, my uncle was able to prop himself up and sit beside his daughter.

"Who gives away this woman?"

"I do."

The whole family is here now. Erica is in her white linen dress, and the flowers from the bouquets are in water. And we stand around my uncle, holding hands—Anushka in the sling across Yvette's chest and my aunt combing my uncle's hair with her fingers. Archer's chasing my father outside, their red shirts darting back and forth through the window, and one by one, we tell my uncle that we love him and we're here.

He smiles and opens his eyes and looks at all of us, and when we kiss him, he kisses back. And now and then, he goes back to fly-fishing like he has done all week, casting his rod toward the end of the bed, where his daughters and my nana sit.

"Did you get a good one?" we ask.

He shakes his head and tries again as the family closes in around him, and suddenly this doesn't feel like death at all. This feels like life. The room tightens with the flexed muscle of the human spirit and all its empowerment and love. Hands clasp together like a chain. Sisters embrace.

We stay by my uncle's bed through the afternoon and the night, watching a master fly-fisherman cast his imaginary rod toward the vases of stargazer lilies, our fading voices rooting him on, even after he catches his fish and goes to fly.

In the days that follow my uncle's passing, laughter and the exchange of stories are wedged between tears and hugs, extraordinary moments of a life lived so fully that it is impossible to think anyone ever really disappears. How can it be possible when we share such bold memories of the people left behind, reenacting their lives in conversation and the songs we sing that remind us?

Edelweiss, Edelweiss. Every morning you greet me.

It is clear as we're singing that Uncle Pete is with all of us, folded between our fingers as we hold each other's hands, uncapping our mason jars of memories, releasing the butterflies in our hearts.

When the dinner table is cleared and clean, we settle side by side in the living room. My sister seats herself at the piano, and Archer finds his favorite spot on the floor below my parents' couch to play with his toys. He babbles matter-of-factly as he tries to figure out how to build the tallest block skyscraper he can without risking its fall. Anushka coos, peeking out from the space between Aunt Fran's arms. And I think about how incredible it is that little people can come into the world and bring so much joy. How the wonder and innocence of children is enough to renew faith in a widow and youth in the elderly, and bring life to a family mourning death.

Nana leans over and whispers quietly to Archer, waiting for his face to show signs of recognition. She looks like a child beside him, giggling and smiling. She watches him build a new world out of blocks, a world we all exist within, as keepers of tales past and creators of stories to come—generations of characters and eccentrics who share the same insurmountable love.

I hold Nana's hand, and we watch Archer together in silence, seeing him differently, loving him in the same way. Because suddenly it all makes sense. We enter this world with voices echoing the sentiments of our relatives—a judge with glasses down upon his nose, a fly-fisherman caught in the hearts of all who adored him, their recycled spirits reflecting the light in all of our eyes, alive in stories told and passed on through generations like heirlooms.

We are all better for knowing Archer. We are all bigger-hearted and optimistic and brimming with hope. My mother and my father and Nana, who whispers all of her secrets into his ear. My sister, who plays him the flute as he watches her with glowing eyes, and my brother, whom he resembles most of all. My grandparents, who gaze at him smiling, and Hal's brother and parents, who travel thousands of miles just to hold his hand across the street. And then there are the beloved ghosts who haunt our hearts like angels.

"It brings me pleasure to know that somewhere in that super delicious little boy, some genes of mine are banging around," Hal's father recently wrote me. "Certainly, I have to acknowledge the contributions of so many others, the long line of donors that stretch from this world to the next, but nonetheless, it is a happy moment to realize that with all the others, I'm in there too."

Perhaps this is why I search Archer's face, looking for myself. Does he have my eyes? My laugh? Because being "in there" means being a part of him always. And nothing can change that, not for me or any of Archer's relatives.

No one really knows what happens when we die, but I like Nana's theory: that the inner voices we hear aren't necessarily our own but the crackling embers of past lives still present, alive in the voices of a family who gathers around the dinner table and laughs all the way through dessert.

Everything is relative, after all.

SPECIAL NEEDS

"DOES HE HAVE any words yet?" our pediatrician asks at Archer's two-year appointment.

"No."

"Not any? Six months ago, you said he had a few words."

"I know. . . . "

I'd lied to her at the last appointment. I was afraid of what that meant for us. I figured he would get there on his own. Just like he did with his other delayed developmental milestones, crawling at thirteen months and walking at seventeen. I told myself to wait until he turned two. *He'll surely be talking by then,* I thought. For the past six months I've tried everything I can think of to get Archer to talk. But still no words. No "Mama." No "Dada." No nothing.

"He doesn't have words. Not a single one," I admit.

"I see," she says, scribbling away on her clipboard. Big illegible scribbles that I can't read upside down.

I tighten my arms around Archer and repeat to myself over and over not to worry.

"He's just a late bloomer," I explain. "He's always done things on his own time."

That's okay! That's good! That is how it should be!

And then the words I have been dreading.

"I'd like him to see a therapist. Run some tests. Don't worry," she says. "I'm sure everything's fine."

I have had my fair share of therapists, having sought help for myself on many occasions, but Archer is so young. *Too* young. I just don't see the point.

She hands me a piece of paper. "Call this number. They will come to your house, and guess what? It's free."

EARLY INTERVENTION, it reads.

"Okay," I say, but inside I am screaming, *No! Fuck you! No! Leave him alone! Give him time! He's fine! He's perfect! He doesn't need anyone to talk to him or test him or teach him! Fuck you! Fuck all of you!*

On the way home, I reluctantly make the call. "We'll send you some paperwork and go from there," the voice on the line says.

When I think of intervention, I think of someone trying to break up a fight, changing the course of events—but why would I want to change anything? Why would I want to change Archer?

It's just a therapist, Bec, I tell myself.

It's just a therapist.

Since the beginning of my pregnancy, I have been adamant

about doing it all myself. I don't believe in waiting lists or classes or private education. I believe in living. And showing my child the way to do so passionately. I hate tests. I fight with teachers. I tolerate doctors. And as a parent, I have trusted that I am the one who knows what's best for my child. I know what Archer needs, and I can and should be able to give it to him.

Until now I haven't been worried about what Archer "should" be doing because I see how happy he is wandering around on his own.

He's on his own path . . .

And we have all enjoyed watching him.

"Whatever we need to do," I hear myself say to the voice on the phone.

And suddenly I am vulnerable—forced to stuff my "Fuck the man" attitude in my back pocket and do as I am told. Opening my house to a stranger so that she can teach my son to speak because I can't. I must go against his natural developmental clock because it isn't functioning "normally," and that is cause for concern.

All this time, I have been telling myself that everything is fine. But what if I've been wrong? I have purposely kept myself away from web pages that might suggest otherwise.

Oh god . . . he's obsessed with spinning things. He's in his own world. He wanders aimlessly, talking to the clouds. Laughing.

There is no possible way I could love my child more, no possible way I could love him any less. And even though I've been told that nobody is perfect, I beg to differ. Archer *is* perfect. He always will be. No matter what. Just the way he is. Even if he is slowly making his way down the path, kicking stones and hugging trees as his peers speed by. He will get there. Wherever he's going. I only hope I can guide him as best as I can, that I can be open to specialists and therapists and all the "ists," if need be. Because for whatever reason, that is what is scariest to me—seeking help when I feel like I'm the one who should be giving it.

I watch the therapist's van pull up to the curb through the gap in the curtain. She gets out of her car, organizes her things, and checks our address against her notes. I close the curtain and go to the door.

She is our first specialist. There will be two more in the next week: a speech therapist and a developmental specialist. But first, her.

"Knock, knock!" she calls through the screen. She has kind eyes and a clipboard. I introduce myself and Archer and invite her in.

"I'm here to ask you a lot of questions, is all," she assures. "I'll make it painless."

Too late. I'm already hurting. We should be at the park right now. We should be nibbling crackers in the sand.

"Great," I lie.

She takes a seat on the couch so I sprawl out on the floor.

"Do you want anything to drink?" I ask.

"No thank you."

I pick at my nail polish.

Stop picking at your nail polish.

I can't help it. It's flaking everywhere.

She starts down her list of questions. I answer her quietly. Honestly.

She asks about my pregnancy and Archer's birth and his development. When he sat up for the first time. When he started to crawl. When he walked. How he communicates with us.

"Does he point? Does he wave? Does he hug?"

"Yes. Yes. Yes," I say. "But only when he wants to."

She nods and writes something down.

Archer reaches toward a cup of water. I hold it to his lips as he drinks.

"Can he hold it himself?"

"Sometimes."

"Does he use a spoon and fork?"

"Sometimes."

She looks me dead in the eye when she asks me questions. It makes me want to look away. I go back to picking my nails, and she goes back to watching Archer. I want to read her thoughts. *What is she thinking?*

"What is your top level of education?" she suddenly asks.

I hate this question. It has nothing to do with anything. It says nothing about me or my intelligence. It says nothing about my work ethic. And surely, it says nothing about Archer.

"Actually, I decided that college wasn't for me," I say. "I explored other options." I feel the need to justify my decision to skip college and go straight to work. I have always been an autodidact, preferring to take night courses at UCLA when I wanted to know more about art history, or Otis College when I wanted to learn photography. "My formal education says nothing about me. I'm informally taught," I say defensively. Except there's no option for that on her questionnaire.

"So you're high school educated."

I swallow.

"I'm high school educated," I repeat back to her, knowing that means something to her on her sheet of notes and statistics. Just like Archer's inability to speak. And I think about how someone will go down her list of notes and think they know me. Someone will go down her list of notes and think they know Archer.

"My husband finished college," I say.

Why do I have to be so sensitive? She has to ask these questions. It isn't up to her. It's on her sheet. She's doing her job. But I know she is here to make an assessment. What I say matters. Everything matters.

I cross my arms. I become paranoid, *Fear and Loathing in Los Angeles*, and I pace the room as Archer runs around in circles over and over, screaming and laughing.

He never runs around in circles like this, and suddenly I'm obsessed with the clipboard and her smiling eyes. She watches him and takes notes, and I wonder if his running around in circles is "bad" or "not normal" or "cause for concern."

Circles. He runs in circles, I imagine she is thinking. *And his mother has a high school education, nothing more.*

I feel very small, like a little girl who has to restrain herself from running in circles too.

Hours seem to pass. I answer all of her questions. I don't know what my answers mean, but I answer them all the same. I pretend I am comfortable with her in my house. She's a nice woman and I feel terrible for not wanting her here. But I can't help it. I want her to leave. Now.

"He stacks blocks and spins wheels and smells every flower," I tell her, and I love that he does these things but I'm not sure if I should. She nods and checks another three boxes on her sheet.

"I don't think anything is wrong," I say. "Archer's very different. He's special. He's not like the other children, but it's by choice. It's because he is unique. I want him to realize that. I want him to grow up knowing what a beautiful thing it is to be different. I don't want him to follow the leader or feel more comfortable in a crowd than he does on his own. I want his growth to be organic. Hormone-free," I say.

"He will always be Archer, but therapy is a great help for those who need a little push. And it's free of charge," she says. "It will help him, that's all."

Hormone-free, I think.

"It helps," she says.

And I don't know who to believe—myself or this stranger with kind eyes.

"I guess we'll just wait to hear back and decide what to do from there," I say.

I sign a stack of paperwork. Archer's name is spelled incorrectly, and I wonder if it's a sign. She doesn't know him. She doesn't even know his name.

Shut up, I tell myself. *Just give it a chance. Just see what they have to say.*

I thank her for her time. Archer waves goodbye, and through the curtains we watch her drive away and out of sight.

"I think we should do it," Hal says after the second therapist arrives and insists speech therapy is the way to go.

"He should be talking by now. I think it would be beneficial for him to meet with a therapist a couple times a week," she told us as Archer sat beside her, trying to blow bubbles by sticking the wand to his nose and making *shhhhhh* sounds.

I liked her, but I don't want to make any decisions yet.

"I think this is bullshit," I argue.

"Maybe Archer needs a little help with his words; help we can't give him," Hal continues.

"But we're his parents!"

"But they're professionals!"

"Our parents didn't have 'professionals'! Their parents didn't have 'professionals.' Children weren't diagnosed for being 'different,' for not being like everyone else! I will not allow Archer to be categorized or diagnosed as anything other than 'Archer.' I just won't!"

"Bec, calm down. You're scared. It's okay to be scared."

I burst into tears. "I'm not scared!"

But I am scared. I'm scared that my decisions will affect Archer's life. Every decision I make from here on out will have repercussions. Making my own mistakes is one thing. Making Archer's is another.

"I just don't want this 'intervention' to lead to other interventions until Archer doesn't have a mind of his own anymore."

"Bec, Archer is fine."

"What happened to parents going with their gut? Acting on instinct?"

"What's your instinct?"

"That Archer doesn't need intervention."

But I'm too afraid to admit that maybe it isn't instinct I am acting on. Maybe it's just impossible for me to see my son in any other way but my own.

≈ ✼ ≈

When I was three years old I refused to say I was sorry. I refused at four, five, and even six—my reasoning being, "Why should I say I'm sorry if I'm not sorry? I didn't do anything wrong." My mom fought me on this issue for years until eventually I gave in. Because whether I meant it or not was beside the point. People say they're sorry even when they're not. Because it's the right thing to do. Because it's kind.

I played the piano for many years. But it was Bach, not Bec, so I quit. Because I couldn't read music as well as I could play by ear. Because I wanted to arrange everything myself. And I refused to practice any other way.

I may have been a total pain in the ass, but that was the risk I was willing to take. I knew what I wanted, and couldn't do something I didn't love. I acted without hesitation, on impulse, and always from a place of personal truth.

When I disagreed with an assignment in school, I refused to do it, backing up my reasons with five-page essays, even if the assignment was to write a paragraph. *Write a paragraph about why it's important to tell the truth.* I earned zeros on multiple occasions for some of my best work. I made up for low scores with extra credit to maintain my A average and keep my AP courses. Compromise. Breaking rules to prove a point was always more important to me than following rules and having no point at all. Because what's the point . . . if there's no point?

Several years ago I was almost arrested for kidnapping a friend on his birthday. Some idiot drove by and saw us carrying our friend to our car with a sweatshirt over his face, and the SWAT team showed up minutes later. Gun to my head, I managed to say two words to the officers who had cuffed me and flattened me against the asphalt in my party dress: "Fuck you."

I didn't even know I said it. It slipped out. I realize now the level of stupidity and blame myself for having had to endure fifteen minutes with my face in the concrete. I like to think I learned a valuable lesson from the experience: Shut the fuck up when an officer pulls his weapon. But I also learned a valuable thing about myself: I'm not afraid when I know I'm innocent. Or in the right. Or not doing anything wrong. I am so confident with my decisions that even a man in a badge with a weapon doesn't scare me. And knowing that was liberating.

Today is Archer's final evaluation with the developmental specialist, who explains to Hal and me—after spending twenty minutes on the floor with Archer and several diagrams and building blocks—that he has a severe case of My Way or the Highway Syndrome. In other words, he's a giant pain in the ass, like me.

"He doesn't want to do what he is told. He's rebelling. Already," she says.

Archer places the blue circle on the black square and the red triangle on the green rectangle and laughs uncontrollably when the specialist tells him, "No. You have to do it *this* way."

Archer shakes his head and pouts.

My way or the highway.

He doesn't want to. He isn't sorry. Or afraid. Or eager to impress. He has his own ideas. He wants to write his own paper. He's telling her politely, in his Archer way, to fuck off.

My first thought is, *Come on, dude. Just put the green triangle on the green triangle . . . for Mommy. Please?*

But then she says something that changes my mind.

"Archer. I know you don't want to, but you're going to have to learn how to conform if you want to get anywhere in this world, bud. . . ."

Oh no . . . she didn't just say that. . . .

She turns to me. "He must eventually learn to do as he is told. That's the world we live in, unfortunately. That's the only way to succeed. I'm afraid if we don't intervene, Archer might become the 'problem child' in school, and trust me, you don't want a problem child."

I'm twisting my face so hard I start to laugh. When I'm angry, I cry, and when I'm really angry, I laugh. It's like my emotions get jumbled up or something. The specialist flashes me a look like I'm some kind of anarchist for thinking she is funny. For thinking Archer's "problems" are a laughing matter.

She has just proved what I have been afraid of all along, that parents are made to think their children are problematic if they are individuals. *Get in line. Take a number. Do what you are told, even if and when you disagree.*

No. That is not the world we live in. That is how we are *told* we must live in order to get by, and unfortunately, no one wants to speak up anymore. Is it possible that "no child left behind" is just a gentler way of saying that no child will have the freedom to wander away?

I stop laughing. "Actually, no. Conformity is not the *only* way to succeed."

Because "getting by" is not what life's about. Aspiring for mediocrity and doing what we are told is not what we should teach our children. Conforming is not the answer to Archer's developmental "differences." Or anyone's, for that matter. If our kids are the future, for god's sake, let's teach them to question *and let them lead the way.* Following the leader has never been a way to make any positive change.

I know Archer is special. He has an instinctual independence that has enabled him to create his own language, regardless of the fact no one can understand him. He knows what he wants. He does his own thing.

Growing up, I was lucky to have parents who enabled me to be myself, teaching me the value of compromise but never the laws of conformity. I would have rebelled against them if they had. I would have run away. Just like I know Archer will do if I or anyone else tries to put him in a box.

Archer waits for the specialist to move to her next test, a piece of wood with four pegs, before placing the shapes in the *right* place.

I have agreed to put Archer in speech therapy because Hal is right, he should probably know some English if he plans on doing anything extraordinary for America (or any other English-speaking country). I have no idea what else the specialists will recommend when we get his report: a "green-on-green class" or whatever they offer these days to teach toddlers to sit quietly with different colored piles of shapes. I do know we have a choice in the matter. There is always a choice.

"Let's wait and see. . . . "

The doctors and specialists are right. Archer does have special needs. Every child does. It is that specialness that leads to individualism and greatness. Child classification should not be a prerequisite for class. So long as we are guiding our future leaders toward sheepsville, we cannot complain about the current state of our society.

In a way I am grateful to the "ists" and their tests and questions and all the information. It's nice to know there are options, but even more so, it's nice to know there is the option to say no.

Of course you have to know the rules before you break them, and Archer will certainly know rules. But he will also make his own. And I will make sure he knows that although conformity is *a* way to get by in this world, it has never been *the* way to excel.

And I won't be sorry for saying so.

NO SACRIFICE

"LET THE BABY adapt to you," were the first words my grand-mother said to me when I told her I was pregnant.

"Okay," I answered without thinking too much about it. Her comment caught me off guard. I had expected a gasp on the other end of the line, but instead her words were strong. "You want the baby to adapt to your schedule, Rebecca, and it will. Babies are very adaptable little people."

She repeated this same advice to me whenever I saw her.

"Remember . . . " she would say, concerned that I would forget.

When Archer was born she stopped. Perhaps she had figured her pep talk was no longer needed. Or maybe she could see that I was naturally following her advice.

Archer is in his bedroom as I write this. And I am in mine, cross-legged on my bed with the air conditioner on. I am working on this book, and he is looking at one: *Where the Wild Things Are*. A page is torn out toward the end of the story, when Max decides it's time to go home because he misses his mother. The page disappeared one day. Sometimes Archer tears pages out of his books and hides them behind the bookshelf. The other day I found twelve pages and a dozen stale Cheerios flattened against the wall, ridden with dust and dog hair. I thought of stapling together a book out of the misfit pages, but then remembered staples aren't childproof, so I threw the pages away.

I lean over the side of the bed and peek at Archer through his open bedroom door. He's arguing with the wild things and shaking his head. He doesn't see me watching him. He's in his own world, so I go back to mine.

I type madly while I still can, finishing my allotted hour of work before it's playtime again. A walk to the park, perhaps, or maybe we'll play in the hose like we did yesterday, but first I must finish this chapter. I'm almost done. *So close.*

Archer is my Max, I think. He needs his time with wild things so I can have time with mine, with the creatures that crawl all over my brain looking for an exit so they can finally be free.

And somehow, without saying so, he understands that I have other priorities besides him. I can't be just his mother. There are characters that need looking after. There are projects and all kinds of ideas. He turns the page. *Let the Wild Rumpus start!*

One of my biggest fears about becoming a mother was that I would wake up passionless, unable to dig my fingers into my own flesh for ideas. Vacant of thought, my ambitions might quickly be forgotten, my insides erased of their contents to make room for Archer in an already cluttered interior. I have always loved myself most when writing. My confidence peaks when my right hand takes hold of a pencil or my fingers click the keys of my laptop. I was afraid this feeling would go away, that I would be so consumed with mother-hood, I would forget my original hood: myself.

I have always defined myself as a writer first. Before I was a woman and a wife and a mother and a friend, I was a little girl who wrote. Before I knew how to write I was telling stories. I had to. It was like breathing. The characters I created mir-rored my truths and all the things I was unable to say aloud or admit to myself. I was too shy. Too embarrassed. When inspira-tion struck I was left ecstatic, sometimes for weeks, grasping a "Eureka!" moment and writing for hours, fingers calloused and keys broken from typing so hard. Working through the night to meet a self-imposed deadline was gratifying. I looked forward to all-nighters, a pot of fresh coffee and a carton of cigarettes in the freezer, and I would write until I couldn't see. I still do. Because the stories are happening in my head, and to fight them is to fight myself, to cut off a limb and become asymmetrical. Without my writing, I would be spiritually handicapped, and Archer would surely slip from my one-armed grasp.

Let the baby adapt to you.

Too many times I have heard stories about women who "sacrificed it all" to have children. *I dropped out of school for you. I left my dreams behind for you. I broke myself in half and gave both sides . . . to you.* This frightened me until Archer was born and I realized that a child is not a sacrifice, that unfaithfulness to one's desire is a choice, with or without children or a full-time job to make ends meet. Making a choice to stay home is one thing, but going against every personal need is something very different. The only way we can properly take care of our children is by taking care of ourselves first. *Start within, and work outward.*

Becoming a mother means splitting yourself in two. Squeezing new life from between two walls and becoming half mother, half self. But I believe there is room enough in every woman for passion and work and dreams and her children, for everything she wants with room for dessert. Life is long.

But there is never any time!

One always finds time in her life for what she loves. Like the time I had a boyfriend who lived on the other side of the world, and I stayed up all night to talk to him because his voice lit a fire in me where practicality had no place. It didn't matter that I had to get up early to go to work. Nothing mattered but the joy and sensuality of the moment. Time was no object, and sleep was hardly necessary. I was high on the sound of his voice in the same way that I buzz watching words swarm the computer screen when I get an idea and must drop everything to write it down. I think of our late-night conversations often when I hear the words "There is no time," because it isn't true. Anyone who says so doesn't want it bad enough.

A child is not an excuse for a mother's fading ambition. A child is a huge responsibility, yes, but so is a dream. So is every goal we give ourselves, every wish we make on glow-in-the-dark stars.

Martyrdom does not bring into the world children with a strong sense of self. A mother who sacrifices her livelihood for her children is risking not only her own loss of identity but also the well-being of her children. No child deserves to be resented. It *is* possible to do it all well.

Let the baby adapt to you.

The lessons we teach our children we should also remember to tell ourselves.

"Follow your dreams."

"Be yourself."

"Listen to your heart."

"I believe in you."

Parenthood is not amnesia. One doesn't wake up and forget where she has come from or who she is. Once upon a time, none of us were parents, and that matters for something. All of the things we used to do matter—going to rock concerts and traveling the world and one-night stands and falling in and out of love and pursuing ideas and projects and a life. Bringing a child into the world shouldn't mean locking ourselves out of our own. Nothing will be lost on those who explore their passions limitlessly.

Parenting, like life, is about choice.

Let the baby adapt to you.

I choose to live in a city because city life moves me: the smells and the colorful characters and the flashing lights and the sidewalk cafés—where things get old and are restored instead of knocked down, and strip malls wouldn't dare show their drywall faces. I love watching Archer smile and clap his hands, running wild across the stars on the sidewalk. Here is what feels like home, where Archer can walk to the local museum when he's old enough, passing street musicians on gum-stained corners on his merry way.

Let the baby adapt to you.

I know that the only way Archer will find his way is by watching me find mine. And sacrificing my taste and work and lifestyle sets a poor example for future generations of children who will look to their parents as people, not just as mom or dad.

Having a family is a choice. Happiness is the most underrated accessory to success. It is paramount to be inspired by life in order to be an inspiration to a child.

Let the baby adapt to you.

Archer puts down his book and scampers to my bedside. I empty a box of finger puppets on the bed beside me and remove my headphones.

I explain to him that I'm writing a book about us and that I need just a few minutes and then I promise I'll play him a song on the guitar about monsters and poop and poop-monsters. He has become a fan of my freestyle guitar jams, delighting in my lyrical twists and turns, featuring the Diaper Genie and its hovering stench. *Poop, there it is!* Archer recently took up keyboard, pounding the rainbow keys fervently and laughing at my nonsense, throwing a few wails in there for good measure. A proper bandmate he has become.

"Twenty minutes and we'll rock out, okay?"

Archer babbles something in response, shrugs, and slides down off the bed with two handfuls of finger puppets.

"Rarrrrr!" he growls, running back to his room, spilling his puppets on Max and the wild things.

Let the baby adapt to you.

And I maximize my page on the computer screen, turn up my iTunes, and write on until it's time for band practice. A laptop in exchange for a Fender Stratocaster—slightly out of tune to suit our squeaking voices, and so loud the neighbors will have to close their windows.

"A one, a two . . . a one, two, three four!"

TIDES
and Change

ARCHER IS ON my father's lap and they're reading Archer's favorite book—*The Very Quiet Cricket*—for the sixteenth time tonight, not including the several dozen times they read it this morning and then again this afternoon. My dad's voice changes with each character he reads, and his eyebrows dance above his eyes like fuzzy caterpillars.

But nothing happened. Not a sound. . . .

Over and over my dad reads—a hundred thousand times with as much enthusiasm as the first, and Archer listens quietly. When the book closes, Archer opens it again. I don't have the patience my father has. I get frustrated with the same story over and over.

"Come on, dude! Can't we read something else! *Please?*"

But my dad keeps reading happily, never once checking his watch, even though he has work to do.

But nothing happened. Not a sound. . . .

Archer blinks at the pages with the same curious eyes he's had since the first time I opened the book and read its words aloud.

"Do you want me to take over?" I ask.

"Or I can," Hal offers.

But my dad shakes his head.

"No way! This is Grandpa time."

There is a lot to be said for patience. It's what *The Very Quiet Cricket* is about—waiting until the time is right to make a sound, being able to step away from the complications of life to enjoy the simple moments. Something that has always come naturally to my father, something I am learning how to do. Because the greatest joys are always in the smallest things. Like bedtime stories that never end and fuzzy caterpillar eyebrows that bend and dance. And when you least expect it . . .

. . . Then he rubbed his wings together one more time. And this time he chirped the most beautiful sound that she had ever heard. . . .

"Hi."

"Hi?"

"Hi."

"Did he just say hi?"

"It sounded like it."

"Hi! Hi! Hi!" Archer says, waving frantically at all of us, the friendliest guy in the room, and we all gasp and dance around him like groupies, waving like a bunch of idiots until our excitement fades and Archer stops waving and it's time for him to go to bed.

I park my car in front of my favorite coffee shop, the place I spent many a night during my high school days, studying and writing and nursing cappuccinos with boyfriends and afterward hanging over the bluffs to watch the sea lions huddle in the moonlight on the cove below Prospect Street.

I haven't been here in years, but Archer's old enough to appreciate the sea lions. I carry him down the hill toward the ocean.

I grew up with sand between my toes, chasing the ocean foam with my siblings and cousins, digging for sand crabs when the tide receded. I caught a sea bass with my bare hands when I was ten. The ocean was my summer home. My bare feet had the reefs memorized; I knew when to kick my legs to the surface or swim under the waves so my feet didn't tangle in the rock. I caught flecks of gold in my T-shirt, pretending I was panning with the 49ers. I made necklaces out of shells and collected sand dollars in a jar on my bed stand. Sometimes I would swim far beyond the surf and float on my back in the sun.

It was hard not to be humbled by the crashing waves and the glimmer of silver waters stretching as far as the sky and beyond. As a child, it seemed the ocean was endless, and when the seagulls lifted off and flew west over the Pacific after a long day of slurping sand crabs, I couldn't help but think they were just like me, going home to somewhere pleasant after a day of splashing the ocean with sandy feet.

Roots grow deep beneath the sand, like the buried treasure the old men pursue with their metal detectors.

I lift Archer so he has a better view of the beach below the bluffs, where the sea lions play. Maybe this isn't the first time, but I can't remember ever seeing so many babies, each one by its mother's side.

"Look, Archer! Mommies and babies!"

Archer holds his hand out and smiles, and drags me down the stairs toward the beach. He wants to get closer, so we seat ourselves on the last step and watch them play. The mothers nuzzle their calves on the shore before pushing off awkwardly to the water, flapping around on their bellies toward the sea. Diving under the tiny waves, flipping themselves around coral and kelp.

Archer leaps out of my lap and runs screaming toward them, fearlessly. I run after him, grabbing him by the arms and spinning us in circles until we fall in the sand like two wild animals, barking along with the happy beasts that play hide-and-go-seek behind the rocks.

I know motherhood is supposed to make me feel more grown up, or at least that's what I've been told, but here with the sun in my face and little hands tangled in mine, I feel like I did when I was little: in the moment. Because of Archer, because I'm in love with my son and it is impossible not to take advantage of moments like these when shared with such a wild and wayward soul.

"On our feet, little man. Let's keep walking. There is so much to see."

The clouds hang over the beach like a blanket, but it is still cold. Archer looks up at me and explains in his own language something about the sand and the way it feels between his toes. I can understand him more lately because he uses his hands. He points to his toes or grabs his feet and falls over, or takes my face in his hands and points my nose toward the sky.

Helicopters zoom overhead, back and forth along the shore between the San Diego Bay and Camp Pendleton, and Archer waves.

"Hi," he says, confidently. "Hi. Hi. Hi. Hi. Hi."

He says "hi" to the seagulls and the children who scurry past him like mice. He says "hi" to the old couples holding hands and the surfers shivering in their wet suits.

Archer walks me toward the ocean, slowly at first, and soon picking up speed. He suddenly lets go of my hand and goes sprinting toward the water, splashing and squealing. And then, after a moment, he turns and returns to me. I am his base. *You are safe now.*

I pull him up, and we stay like that for a second before he peels my arms from around his waist and drops down to the ground again, running full speed away from me, toward the lifeguard tower. He burrows his toes in the sand and looks around, taking notes with his knowing eyes, watching as the girls pull their shirts over their heads and chase each other down to the water.

"Eeeek! It's cold!" they scream.

Archer smiles and looks back at me. He knows it's cold too.

And even though everything has changed in the world of sea foam and sandcastles, the landscape here is much the same, an ocean of possibilities and dinged surfboards and the people who walk the shorelines and chase their children joyfully across a landscape speckled with the same gold I panned for when I was Archer's age.

Archer howls like a pup and darts back and forth, making wide circles in the sand as he goes, dizzying himself until he falls down in a heap of kelp. He gets up and does it again, over and over until he becomes distracted by a surfer with his board balanced on his head. He follows the teenage boy to the edge of the sand before he notices the water rushing up again, sending him squealing toward me once more. *Safety.* But only for a second. He slithers down my chest and scurries off, again, to race down the beach, his laughter overlapping with the *cah! cah!* of the seagulls. And I follow his footprints with my own. I place my large bare feet over his tiny ones and dart after him until they're all squished together, until you can hardly tell which feet belong to whom, even though his are so incredibly small.

We run until we're out of breath, until the sun falls down and the tide pushes up along the shore, washing our prints away: disappearing ink upon an endless canvas of particles and a trillion teensy rocks.

We quickly dress and make our way up the rocks toward the parking lot, where my car overlooks the rising tide. I strap Archer in his car seat and retrieve my keys from the floor of my mother's mesh beach bag, and we drive the long way home to Los Angeles with sand between our toes.

$$\gg \text{⁂} \ll$$

It's raining when we reach Orange County, and I turn the windshield wipers on. They glide back and forth to the beat of the stereo, and Archer kicks his feet and slouches against the window, trying to touch the droplets on the glass.

Traffic forms, so I try to switch lanes, but every time I merge into a lane that seems to be moving, it suddenly stops. *I should have just stayed in the other lane, dammit.* We stop and go. Speed up and then break. The rain is falling harder now, and Archer watches out the window, even though there isn't much to see. Only cars and grimacing faces and pounding on steering wheels and blinker lights and hazard lights and windshield wipers, all slightly off beat from one another. But Archer enjoys the rain and the brake lights and all the things that slow life down, the circumstances that aren't in anyone's control. The traffic jams.

So I turn up the music and grab an empty water bottle and sing into my makeshift microphone, and Archer watches me and laughs until the car behind me honks because the traffic is moving again. And then I remember the carpool lane has been beside us all along, so I wait for the dotted line to appear, and then cross it, because there are two of us now. Sometimes I forget. Sometimes I drive all the way home in the fast lane, forgetting that we can ride the carpool lane home, or at least until it ends, because eventually it disappears and all traffic must merge right.

I park in front of our house, against the curb and the current of rainwater washing down the street. We're snug and safe inside our car where it isn't wet and I can control the temperature with the push of a button and the windows are sealed tight so Archer can't catch cold.

But he wants to touch the rain.

But it's cold.

But . . .

"Do you want to go play in the rain?" I ask, and Archer puts his hands over his eyes. *Peekaboo.*

I unbuckle him from his car seat, and when I open the door the rain hits us both in the face, and he laughs and wiggles his fingers. We hold hands down the sidewalk and wait for the cars to pass before crossing the street. He doesn't mind the wet, and I remember how when I was little I used to go outside when I was thirsty and open my mouth to the clouds and how my mom would say to me, "Wear a jacket so you don't catch cold."

The puddles are everywhere and Archer leaps into them with two feet and even though I'm soaking wet and annoyed that my hair is sticking to the side of my face and my open-toed shoes are stained with raindrops, I join him. Because it's a lot more fun to say yes. And I start to think maybe it's just as important to cross the lines as it is to draw them. Maybe rocking the cradle on the treetop doesn't have to be dangerous. Maybe breaking bows and splashing puddles in the rain without the umbrella is just as important as building a strong foundation and wearing a sweater when it's cold outside. Because just as I want to teach Archer to be careful, I want him to know to take risks. There is no such thing as messing up if you go with your heart, and it's a whole lot easier to let go and enjoy the ride, singing along with makeshift microphone until the rain goes away or the traffic clears. You can't learn that from a book or the Internet or in an overpriced class or seminar. That you learn from falling on your face in the sand, from spinning the kaleidoscope and splashing puddles in the rain. Wisdom is for sale everywhere we look, but the real answers are inside.

Inside of Archer.

Inside of me.

Inside of all of us.

An old man with a red umbrella scurries by with his little white dog. He smiles at us, and just as he is about to disappear around the street corner my little cricket turns, waves with both hands, and at the top of his lungs chirps, "Hi!"

BACKWARD
and Forward

HAL AND REBECCA sitting in a tree. K-I-S-S-I-N-G. First comes love, then comes marriage, then comes the baby in the baby carriage. . . . Except it wasn't like that for us. Instead we did things backward and inside out and upside down and our own way. We skipped the engagement for the wedding and the marriage for the pregnancy. We climbed over cement walls and shimmied between electric fences and sleepwalked until we woke up with a pearl between our shells.

Wearing an engagement ring would have been weird since we never were engaged. Life happened quickly and we rushed into marriage and parenthood with our whole hearts but very little practical thought and few material items besides baby gear.

"I think it's time to get you a proper ring," Hal said to me several months ago when, for the first time in our relationship, we had sufficient funds for nonessentials, both of us working our asses off to make it out of the red and into the green pastures of financial stability.

I knew the ring was on its way. I knew that it was arriving by FedEx this afternoon and that Hal was working from home today to sign for it. I knew what it looked like because I picked it out, even though Hal was annoyed that it only took me ten minutes.

"You can't fall in love with the first ring you see," he insisted.

"But that's the one I want!"

"Let's keep looking."

"Fine!" I huffed, knowing there was nothing else. When you know, you just *know*.

A month passed and nothing else interested me. Hal would tear pages from magazines boasting rings from De Beers and Tiffany, but nothing was right. Nothing was *me*. They all looked the same—white diamond solitaires with bands in platinum or gold, like every other ring I've ever seen.

"None of these are right. They're not proper representations of marriage."

Hal rolled his eyes. "What ring is a proper representation of marriage?"

"Something with flaws. Something off-color. Something beautiful and strange and unique. Something confusing and funny with contrast and balance: something representative of us."

"You still want the first one, don't you?"

"That ring or nothing at all."

I come home to Hal on his computer, browsing through footage on his laptop. He produces a makeover show on the HGTV network, and today he is working from home. He's in his usual work-from-home attire, Adidas workout pants and bare feet, and I'm in my bikini top and a towel that's slipping off my hip with a sleeping Archer in my arms. And I smell. Like fish and sunscreen and soggy avocado sandwiches.

"How was the beach?" Hal asks, taking my mesh bag from my arm.

"It was beautiful."

"You're beautiful."

"Gross. I'm waterlogged and my hair is full of sandcastles."

"Shut up. I love you."

And then, before I know what's happening, Hal gets down on one knee.

"Rebecca Ruth Woolf?"

"Yes."

"Will you marry me?"

Hal opens the box to reveal the ring, and even though I picked it out and knew it was coming, it feels special. It doesn't matter that I smell disgusting or that I know to the dollar how much the ring cost because I've been listening to Hal argue with the jewelry dealer for weeks. Hal kneeling before me in his sweaty gym clothes is just so incredibly romantic and in so many ways unexpected. Perfectly and completely unexpected.

His eyes sparkle and I whisper "Yes" in his ear, quietly as not to wake Archer. And Hal kisses me, leaning over our son and his damp swim-trunks, and slides the ring on my finger above my scratched wedding band, and we both gasp.

I chose the ring for its symbolism, a rare cognac diamond cut in half and fused with black onyx, the two sides of our marriage, the light and the darkness in both of us, the light and the darkness in me.

Hal takes my hand and leads me down the hall to Archer's room in the back of our home. I carefully place our son in his crib, and he stirs, clutches his blankie, and rolls into the fetal position. His little toes peek out from under his sandy little bottom.

"What do you think?" Hal whispers. "Is it everything you had imagined it would be?"

I examine my ring and see within its cuts and crevices three years of scenes flashing like stills in a slideshow.

Meeting in the coffee shop on Melrose. *Click.*

The road trip we took up the coast. We had no map, no idea where we were going, so we drove until we reached Santa Cruz, where Hal is convinced Archer was conceived among vanilla-scented drugstore candles bought to mask the stench of the motel room we bargained down to $39 a night. *Click.*

Walking the streets of West Hollywood, wondering what the hell we were going to do about my pregnancy. *Click.*

Moving in together, a couple of strangers with nothing but inside jokes and the cash we borrowed from our parents to make ends meet. *Click.*

Holding hands as I pushed Archer out and into the world. *Click.*

Yelling at each other, and how I said I wanted to run away and join the circus. *Click.*

Falling asleep, the three of us overlapping under spit-up stained sheets. *Click.*

This moment, right now, with me in my towel and Hal with the little black ring box in his hand. *Click.*

"Yes," I say. "It's perfect. It's exactly right." Because two halves make a whole, even if they don't match all of the time.

Hal and Rebecca in Archer's room: K-I-S-S-I-N-G. First comes lust. Then comes pregnancy. Then comes love. Then comes marriage. Then comes the baby in the baby carriage. Then comes engagement.

It may not have the rhythm of the original rhyme, but that's alright by me. I twist my ring and it sparkles in the light of Archer's bedroom and everywhere I look there are rainbows.

ACKNOWLEDGMENTS

It can be really lonely for a new mother, especially when trying to establish a like-minded community. I was lucky enough to find mine in the blogosphere. This book would not be possible without the loyalty of my amazing blog readers at Girl's Gone Child and Straight from the Bottle, the community of inspiring parent-bloggers stirring things up in the www. Your support has been paramount in my decision to write this book and my ability to trust myself as a parent. Thank you for opening your hearts to me and for allowing me to open mine.

With bottomless thanks to Sal Glynn, who has masterfully guided my work and career as only a mentor could. Thank you for being there for me always and for selflessly staying up with me nights and holding my hand.

Thank you to my agent, Laura Rennert, for your constant support and awesomeness and for taking me on after our meeting at the Big Sur Writer's Workshop, and to Magnus Toren at the Henry Miller library for bringing me there. This book would not exist without Brooke Warner at Seal Press for believing in me and allowing me the freedom to just *write*. Also mad love to Laura Mazer, for your help and kindness, and of course Andie East, who just plain rocks.

I am most grateful for Insomnia Café for being my office and watering hole for the last eight years, and to all the talented writers who work feverishly between its walls, especially Gabriel Scott and Joe Nava.

A huge debt of gratitude to the Caught in the Draft writing group, including Elizabeth Regan, Mary Pascual, Steven Starkweather, Andrea Strohm, Riley Devoe, Joanne Bamberger, Jennifer Chevais, Wendy O'Donnell, and Vanessa Craft.

Thanks to Liz Gumbinner at Mom-101 for being a big sister to me, Barbara Rushkoff for your sage advice and virtual hugs, and to Dana Robinson for being an incredible friend all along. I am grateful to Neal Pollack for putting up with my bitching and moaning, and allowing me to tag along with him on occasion as a sisterly sidekick in the parent hood.

With many thanks to Alexa Young, Jason King and Tasha Boucher, whose support has been vital to this project and every literary project since the beginning. Eternal hugs to Frank Alvarez for dropping everything at a moment's notice to watch Archer so I could take (many) moments to breathe. You are family. To my oldest friends and fellow new, unexpected mothers—Meredith Becker Toraason and Kendra Strandemo Cullum—I love you both.

Thank you to Charlotte Huang, for allowing me to attach myself to your hip and for being my everyday playmate. To Dana Taylor for overwhelming me daily with your generosity, love, and bitch-slapping when I needed it. Thank you for always telling it like it is—you are the best friend possible.

I am grateful to the writing teachers of my youth, specifically Adele Lapadula, Tim Roberts, and Kevin Leal.

With many thanks to Rachel Fershleiser and Larry Smith and everyone at *SMITH* magazine for telling stories and supporting mine, and to everyone at Babble.com for being my virtual home away from home.

I am forever grateful to the amazing kids and teens at the Starlight Starbright Children's Foundation for their hope and lust for life. Thank you for inspiring me daily for the last four years and showing me what it means to be a good parent, and hopefully, a decent human being. I am deeply thankful for Lauren Henderson for being Archer's surrogate fifteen hours a week and one of my dearest friends, and Scarlett Evans, for being my ultimate hero. You have both taught me so much about the beauty and preciousness of life and how to live in the moment. I knew you both as children and am in awe of the women you have become. Your friendships are rainbows on my heart.

Thank you to my amazing and loving family, including and not limited to my in-laws, Norman and Susan; my grandparents, Patricia and the late Louis Welsh and Betty and Milt Woolf; my aunt Fran and cousins Yvette, Anushka, and of course Erica, who has been my best friend since infancy and my partner in creative blitzkrieg—thank you for reading my early drafts and rooting me on, sister. I love you so much. In loving memory of Peter J. Filanc, who lives on in all of our hearts.

Mad props go out to my dad, Larry, for his raps and rhymes and love for Archer, and for being the kind of father everyone should be so lucky to have. You're like Superman with a mustache. Thank you to my brother, David, a brilliant human and a constant support to me through all of my craziness, and to my sister, Rachel—you amaze me.

Infinite thank yous to my mother, who has read every word I have written since kindergarten, edited this book with me, stayed up nights putting up with my tantrums, held my hand. You are my North Star, my best friend. I want to be like you when I grow up.

And to Hal, my husband and partner, thank you for allowing me to write about us and for loving me anyway, for setting my heart on fire and filling my life with laughter. Most of all, thank you for Archer.

The biggest thanks of all goes to Archer, my muse and heart and home, my pirate of the snails. This book is homage to you and the light you continue to shine on my world and the worlds of so many others. I love you so much.

And to every new mother struggling to balance motherhood with independence, I believe with my whole heart that it is possible to have it all. I hope this book can help in some small way.

© MATT ARMENDARIZ

Rebecca Woolf with son Archer

ABOUT
the Author

REBECCA WOOLF has worked as a freelance writer since age sixteen, contributing to publications including MSN, Nerve.com, Babycenter, *19 Magazine UK, Huffington Post,* and *Grace Ormonde Wedding Style*. Woolf authors the popular parenting blogs Girl's Gone Child and Babble.com's Straight from the Bottle. She lives in Los Angeles with her husband and son, Archer.

289

SELECTED TITLES FROM SEAL PRESS

For more than thirty years, Seal Press has published ground-breaking books. By women. For women. Visit our website at www.sealpress.com, and our blog at www.sealpress.com/blog.

SINGLE MOM SEEKING by Rachel Sarah. $14.95, 1-58005-166-9. A single mom who knows the difference between "going to bed" and "putting to bed" shares her heartfelt and hilarious take on the challenges of balancing motherhood with dating.

DELIVER THIS! by Marisa Cohen. $14.95, 1-58005-153-7. A smart, informative book that helps mothers and mothers-to-be explore the traditional and alternative birthing choices.

FULL FRONTAL FEMINISM by Jessica Valenti. $15.95, 1-58005-201-0. A sassy and in-your-face look at contemporary feminism for women of all ages.

INTIMATE POLITICS: HOW I GREW UP RED, FOUGHT FOR FREE SPEECH, AND BECAME A FEMINIST REBEL by Bettina F. Aptheker. $16.95, 1-58005-160-X. A courageous and uncompromising account of one woman's personal and political transformation, and a fascinating portrayal of a key chapter in our nation's history.

SINGLE STATE OF THE UNION edited by Diane Mapes. $14.95, 1-58005-202-3. A witty and revealing collection not only of what it means to be single, but independent as well.